I GOT TIRED
OF
PRETENDING

I GOT TIRED
OF
PRETENDING

Bob Earll

STEM Publications
Tucson, Arizona

STEM Publications
P.O. Box 8367
Tucson, Arizona 85738

Second Printing: September 1989

Library of Congress Catalogue card number 88-062473

ISBN 0-922641-69-2

*This book is dedicated to
little Bobby, my inner child,
little Christina, my wife's
inner child and to our five
month-old daughter, Alexandra.
May it stop with her.*

*Tom Alibrandi, best friend,
author, talk show host.
The man with whom I have
walked most of these miles.*

*Margie Granach, the woman who
put me on this path and showed
me where to place my feet.*

Contents

There Came a Day

That day
The day I had unknowingly and knowingly feared since I was
a small boy.
The day I had run from all of my life.
You know the day.
The day I couldn't do it any more.

I couldn't put on my suit of armor and go out into the world
and pretend that life didn't affect me.

I couldn't put on one more mask to keep the world from
knowing I was flawed.

I couldn't create one more false, agreeable personality to keep
people from being mad at me.

I couldn't attach myself to one more relationship whose unspoken rule was "If you really love me you will never be in conflict with me."

I couldn't muster up the emotional and physical strength required to try to turn life from its natural rhythm, which is:

into what I believed was necessary for my survival, which is

_____

I couldn't exercise control over one more situation or person.

I couldn't be responsible for one more person's feelings.

I couldn't find the energy to try to change life from reality as is so aptly put by a popular bumper sticker: SHIT HAPPENS to NOTHING HAPPENS THAT SOMEBODY (usually me) ISN'T TO BLAME.

Yet on that day.
You know the day.
I didn't know how to stop!

Introduction

Nine years ago I was earning more money than I had ever dreamed of. I was a successful television writer working on the staff of a hit television show. I lived in a penthouse apartment at the beach. I roller-skated weekends on the Venice boardwalk. I drove a new Cadillac Seville. I was in the process of divorcing a beautiful wife. I had a lovely young girlfriend. And I had accomplished it all on the natch. I hadn't used drugs or alcohol as a means of escape for seventeen years. So you can imagine my surprise when day after day all I wanted to do was lie down somewhere and die.

My girlfriend suggested that I needed help. Believing that women and relationships were my problem, I sought out and found a therapist by the name of Margie Granach.

During the next eight years, under Margie's guidance, I was introduced to my Inner Child. What a frighteningly wonderful experience. I learned that there is a direct relationship between what happened to me as a child and every one of the problems that have plagued me throughout my life. And that the same holds true for most of the people I meet and hear about.

This book is about the experiences I had, the lessons I learned, and the tools I used in order to set myself free from the prison constructed for me by my parents when I was a small child.

This book is not about blame. It's about finding out who's responsible, although yelling, screaming, and blaming, even though directed at an empty chair, was a very necessary part of my gaining freedom.

This book is about doing my family-of-origin work. Which, simply stated, means I went back and found out what *really* happened when I was a child and how it affected my life as an adult. Then, once past the initial rage, anger, and sadness over that information, I went back wherever possible to find out what happened to my parents when they were children. That information gave my heart something to work with when I started the process of trying to forgive my parents.

This book is also about feelings. My feelings. The feelings that began to surface while I was in the process of finding out why, ever since I can remember, I have felt something was wrong with me. That somehow I was flawed and different from other people.

No matter what the situation, no matter how cool I appeared, the truth was that on the inside I knew I wasn't enough. I lived with the nagging fear that someday, somewhere, somehow I would be publicly exposed. A great deal of my energy went into avoiding people and places where exposure was a possibility.

This book is about the front line issues of adult children of alcoholics, adult children from dysfunctional families, and co-dependence. They are, for the most part, the same issue.

The book tells the story of a desperate, frightened, inadequate man meeting a small, frightened, distrustful boy and the two of them doing together what neither of them could do alone. They ride the great, wild, life-changing horse called *truth,* down the road to freedom.

Special Thanks

to
Bill O'Donnell and Mike Mathews

When I first finished an outline and three full chapters for this book, I sent them off to a major publisher, who was supposedly interested in this type of material. Shortly thereafter, I received a letter from the editor telling me why the book wouldn't be acceptable without major changes.

I turned to Mike Mathews, a friend and one of the partners in the company that puts on my workshops and told him I believed in what I had to say and I didn't want to water it down in order to get the book published. He agreed, and the next day he put Bill O'Donnell and me together.

I was aware of Bill O'Donnell and the tremendous job his staff does at Sierra Tucson. Terry Rossiter, a good friend of mine, went through co-dependence treatment at Sierra Tucson two years ago. The last weekend of her stay she was informed her eldest son, young Bill Rossiter, had just been diagnosed with AIDS. Two days later she completed the program on what was young Bill Rossiter's thirty-sixth birthday and her own thirty-eighth wedding anniversary.

xiv / SPECIAL THANKS

With the tools given her in treatment, she was able to take a month to nurture herself, before focusing on the ordeal ahead. What a wonderful gift.

The next year was hope and despair, love and hate, closeness and distance. Then, she and Bill Rossiter senior went to California to spend their son's last few months with him. She found she had the strength and courage she didn't know she had, and I don't mean the stiff upper lip kind. She was able to experience her feelings. She was able to communicate her feelings to her son and to the rest of her family. She was able to help her son to communicate his feelings, his fear, his anger, and his sadness. He passed away on January 26, 1988. Young Bill, you are missed by all of us who knew you.

Terry told me that she had called Tucson numerous times to get continuing support from her counselor. When a staff cares that much, it reflects the beliefs of the person at the top.

Thank you, Bill O'Donnell, for believing so much in me and in the importance of the issue of co-dependence that you agreed, without hesitation, to publish this book. People with your dedication and courage help make a difference.

Most of all, thank you for allowing me to tell my truth, my way.

Acknowledgments

Cy Chermak, who bought my first story and assigned me to write my first script. Jim Miller, who was always there to help me stop the moving camera in my first year as a writer. Audrey, who helped me believe I could do it.

Bob Crewe, friend and Alexandra's godfather. Thank you for your encouragement and support over the years.

Steven Bochco and John Frankenheimer, both of whom had faith in me as a writer and came to my aid as friends.

Cliff Portnoff, Michael Glasser, Peter Nava, Aaron Brownstone, and Tom Kenny, who gave me a much-needed helping hand when things were bleak.

All the people in various twelve-step recovery who have helped me on this journey.

Karen Randall, my editor, who drove me nuts asking "what does that mean?" By the time I would explain in writing what "it" meant, the book had been improved. I thank her for her patience.

GOD.

I am convinced that babies arrive in this world
not only needing love but KNOWING what love is. That
is why it is so painful for them as children and has
such dire consequences for them as adults when they
are raised by emotionally unavailable parents.

Bob Earll

CHAPTER 1

What's Up Doc?

One of the major problems of adults raised in alcoholic or dysfunctional homes is lack of information. So I want to start off by sharing some of the information that has helped me.

There are two kinds of families, functional and dysfunctional.

A functional family is one built on a foundation of love and mutual trust. The parents have a good sense of self. They are in touch with feelings. They are able to express their feelings openly. They are able to let their children express their feelings openly. They are emotionally available for their children. There is an abundance of physical contact, holding, hugging. Rigidity and conformity are discouraged. The uniqueness of each child is encouraged. The parents have clearly defined limits and boundaries. Limits: how far they will go. Boundaries: how far they will let you go.

Dysfunctional families come in many different models. The three most common are alcoholic, workaholic, and the severely strict, rigid models that are usually militarily or religiously fanatic or demanding of perfection from all members. There are many methods used in dysfunctional homes to control the children:

INTIMIDATION: "I'll give you something to cry about;" "Wait till your father gets home;" "God will punish you;" "You'll burn in hell;" "You'll never get into a good school;" "Wait till I get my hands on you." Often the size of the parent looming over the child is sufficient.

FALSE POWER: "If you do, it will kill me;" "You'll be the death of me yet;" "You'll break you mother's heart."

LOUDNESS: yelling, screaming, banging and slamming things around. Children are born with only two fears; the fear of falling and the fear of loud noises. So loudness is common and effective.

BRIBERY: the offering or withholding of love, approval, money, objects, food, privileges, and soforth. "If you don't stop crying (expression of sadness, frustration), you can't go to the movies." "If you don't stop pounding your fists (expression of anger), you can't have your allowance;" "Control yourself or there'll be no dessert."

BLAMING: "It's your fault;" "It's her fault;" "It's his fault;" "It's their fault;" "It's the weather's fault;" "It's my boss's fault."

INSTILLING GUILT: "How could you, after all I've done for you?" "I work my fingers to the bone and this is the thanks I get?" Guilt often comes in the form of a question, that if answered with the truth, will get you killed.

INSTILLING SHAME: "You should be ashamed of yourself;" "Only a terrible person could do something like that;" "Don't ever use that awful word again;" "There must be something very wrong with you;" "Don't touch yourself there."

Adults raised as children in dysfunctional homes are unable to distinguish the difference between shame and guilt. As John Bradshaw puts it: "Guilt means I did something wrong, and I can do something about it. Shame means there is something wrong with me that can't be fixed."

Fossum and Mason describe shame as "an inner sense of being completely diminished or insufficient as a person. It is the self judging the self. A moment of shame may be humiliation so painful or an indignity so profound that one feels one has been robbed of her or his dignity or exposed as basically inadequate, bad, or worthy of rejection. A PERVASIVE SENSE OF SHAME IS THE ONGOING PREMISE THAT ONE IS FUNDAMENTALLY BAD, INADEQUATE, DEFECTIVE, UNWORTHY, OR NOT FULLY VALID AS A HUMAN BEING." I don't have any trouble identifying with that description.

Fossum and Mason go on to describe a shame-bound family as a "family with a self-sustaining, multigenerational system of interaction with a cast of characters who are (or were in their lifetime) loyal to a set of rules and injunctions demanding control, perfectionism, blame, and denial. The pattern inhibits or defeats the development of authentic relationships, promotes secrets and vague personal boundaries, unconsciously instills shame in the family members as well as chaos in their lives, and binds them to perpetuate the shame in themselves and their kin. It does so regardless of the good intentions, wishes, and love which may also be part of the system."

The preceding is only a portion of the methods used and brief descriptions of shame. There are a few good books that cover the material in length, and I've included them in a suggested reading list in the back of this book.

Now it's not too hard to see that by the time the children are two or three years of age most of the damage has already been done. By the time the children are five or six years of age they deny the pain, sadness, and anger they feel at being controlled and oppressed and, in order to survive, become little actors and actresses joining their parents in the family theater.

The play they are performing is a tragedy.

Mommy, because she has no sense of self, is acting out her role of mother and wife according to the script given to her by her parents. Daddy, because he has no sense of self, is acting out his role of father and husband according to the script given to him by his family. The fact that both Mommy and Daddy usually feel inadequate to their roles and fall far short of the performance they expect from themselves is one of the major causes of violence in the home.

The children are assigned roles essentially designed to keep the production running smoothly. Now an adult or a child raised in a functional home, suddenly finding himself thrust upon the stage in a smooth-running, dysfunctional family production, would run in horror.

I am an only child and, like most only children, I found myself playing a variety of parts, each designed to keep peace in the family and to keep me from being killed. In other words, I did my part to keep the production running smoothly.

Children in larger dysfunctional families usually adopt specific roles and devote their energy to mastering them. In dysfunctional families the parents are already acting out the adult version of these roles. Here are some common roles:

SERGEANT YORK/AMELIA EARHART (the hero): held up by the family to prove that the whole family is okay. If you take into consideration that the hero is usually filled with shame, it will give you an idea of the tremendous conflict. The hero's achievements are never enough.

THE BUILDING SUPERINTENDENT (caretaker): fixes, patches, and repairs in order to keep the family wobbling along. Tries to figure out what everybody's needs are and then tries to please them in order to keep the peace. Will make the telephone calls to lie about why family members can't fulfill their obligations. When they get older, this is the adult child every member of the family calls to have them take care of things. Many of those who choose the helping professions (nurses, doctors, therapists, etc.) as a career fall into this and the hero category.

EMMETT KELLY/LUCILLE BALL (the clown, the comic):   tries to use humor to fix what ever is wrong at the moment. Makes jokes to help the family cover up the truth. Comic/clown can be a dangerous role until they get their timing down. Early in their careers comics and clowns can get some terrible beatings.

THE GHOST (lost child):   disappears. They cause no trouble and are rarely seen or heard. They move through the shadows of their homes. As adults, they will continue to sneak through their own homes, afraid to disturb the sleeping giants.

BONNIE AND CLYDE (the acting out child):   is often the chemically addicted child. The one who is always in trouble at school, with the law, with the neighbors, and so on. This child can be a real blessing, if in the process of trying to get this child fixed, the family is lucky enough to stumble upon a competent professional. A knowledgeable professional will know that the whole family is dysfunctional and needs help.

Some of the professionals working in the co-dependence field say that, if left untreated, these children will act out these roles for the rest of their lives. I disagree. It has been my experience that they will act out the role until they run into significant resistance. At that point they will take on a new role to keep the peace. I've seen some comics get quiet and stay quiet (the ghost) when people stopped laughing. I've seen both male and female heroes become Bonnie and Clydes after hooking up with a "life in the fast lane" type. And so on and so on.

Left untreated, which simply means not doing the family-of-origin work, we will spend the rest of our lives acting out some role. For most of us that role will be determined by the current circumstances in our life. We will play whatever part is required to give us a sense (false) that we have control over our own life and the people in it, or whatever part is required to make us feel we fit in and that people like us, or whatever part is required to drive people away and isolate ourselves.

Regardless of the roles I've picked, the parts I've played, I still always felt deep down there was some terrible thing wrong with me. In other words, my performance was never good enough, and that was always a frightening experience because my performance was all I believed I had.

The oppression of a child as described here creates what many professionals label a co-dependent personality, a personality disorder. Other professionals say co-dependence is a disease; still others say it is an addiction. I don't intend to take up that argument here. All I know for sure is that the oppression took place when I was so small that the only option I had was to make the survival choices. These choices became second nature to me. I knew no other way to live. As far as I was concerned, to think about changing was to think about dying, or worse, exposure.

There seems to be almost as many different definitions of co-dependence as there are professionals writing them. But there is a fine thread of agreement that goes something like this – the oppression of a child and the child's feelings retards the development of a self, an identity, a sense of "this is who I am." And an adult who has been raised in such a manner is powered by a belief system of invalid, life-threatening rules and false information.

Yes, the very same rules that saved your life as a child can be lethal to you as an adult. This is one of the main reasons why changing our belief systems, our lives, ourselves, is so difficult. The inner child still perceives the rules as necessary for his or her survival. There were a number of occasions when I would find myself behaving in a way that I knew was detrimental to me as an adult and didn't know why. But I was powerless to stop myself.

An adult raised without a true sense of self is doomed

to a life of frustration, suppressed and repressed feelings, and unresolved grief. I am leaving out the endless addictions to which these adults turn in order to live with the condition.

Anne Wilson Schaef quotes a number of definitions of co-dependence in her book *Co-Dependence – Misunderstood-Mistreated* (the disease concept). There are books on co-dependence by Robert Subby, Charles Whitfield, Melody Beattie, Sharon Wegshceider-Cruse, Janet Geringer Woititz, and a host of others.

In some of the books on co-dependence you will find some crazy making, mixed messages. For example, more than one of the professionals write about how essential it is for professionals, therapists, and counselors to expose their own co-dependence in order to help others. Yet when it comes to themselves, a couple of them either expose nothing at all or relate an incident that is so sterile it wouldn't offend the Pope.

Now in the past that would have been enough reason for me to scream (perhaps more of a mumble – don't think I was recovered enough to scream) that the author was a fraud and toss the book. But before you throw the baby out with the bath water, let me share with you that, in every workshop I conduct, I have books by all the above authors available for the participants to buy. I think that the good information, valuable guidelines for recovery, and shared experiences (if not their own at least their patients') outweighs the confusion they can create in some of us. Also, fear of exposure is one of the core issues with co-dependents, and the authors are not working in one of the more friendly fields. In allowing their books to be published, they risked attack and tremendous ridicule from the traditionalists in their profession.

Perfection is not available to us. It doesn't exist. But progress is available and does exist. The information presented in these books will help almost anyone progress in the treatment of co-dependence.

CHAPTER 2

"The Truth Will Set You Free"

Long before I started therapy and began to do my family-of-origin work, the truth was calling to me. I just didn't know what it was.

I was going along with my life and, for the most part, thought I was happy. What made that belief possible was that I was out of touch with my feelings. In order to avoid the pain of the truth, my feelings had been shut down since I was a small child. I hadn't experienced real happiness or real sadness on a feeling level. So the conclusion that I was happy held up as long as I continued to ignore the constant stirrings inside.

It was like someone inside me was screaming at me to wake up, someone trapped in a cave-in yelling out, hoping the rescuers will hear. But I had no idea how to listen, who was screaming, what the screams meant, or what to do. I was afraid. So I went along plotting the course of my life with what I believed to be God's help. In reality I was very much like a ball in a pinball machine, painfully ricocheting from one bumper to another to another. And every time I started to roll for that dark mysterious hole that my intuition told me was feelings and freedom – my parents' hands (what happened to me in my childhood) would launch the flippers into action and propel me back out there to score more points – write a script for a more popular TV show so they could tell the relatives, buy a better car, move to a better address, find a prettier girlfriend. "Prettier" meant one not in conflict with my mother.

There were other times when I felt as though I had gotten into the caboose car on a train, and way up there somewhere was an out-of-control engine yanking me through life. I believed that if I could get to the engine and get my hands on the controls everything would be okay.

Still other times I felt as if I were in a circular maze going around and around only to always wind up back at the same spot. Other people were in the maze with me, but they were all going fast, talking loud, and acting as if they knew the way out. Their bravado (denial) made me feel weak, inadequate, and flawed. It never dawned on me that every time I wound up back at the starting point they were all right there beside me.

Over the years I had eliminated alcohol, drugs, red meat, coffee, sugar, and cigarettes from my life, and the screams started getting louder. The pain of the bumpers was becoming unbearable, and I was getting dizzy and sick in the maze. It was the truth calling out to me, trying to tell me this is not how life is meant to be.

I've since learned the screams were the little boy inside of me, crying out in the hopes that, if I would take the time to meet him, I would stop doing to him what my parents had done to him, and he would have a chance at life as God intended it to be. The inner child in all of us understands that "it's never too late to have a happy childhood."

The engine on the train is my being yanked through life by a belief system filled with lies. It is the co-dependent's need for control. I had to work my way up the engine one emotional car from my past at a time. Once in the engine, I learned that freedom from pretending comes not from getting control but from giving it up.

The pinball machine and the maze were what my life was like when trying to live controlled by rules and lies from the past. Bob Subby explains it as "trying to take information from the past and apply it to today where it has no relevance." In both the pinball machine and the maze I knew there was a way out. I knew that if I could find the right person (girlfriend) she could lead me out. I had no idea the person would turn out to be my therapist. Fortunately for me she didn't lead me out; she gave me a map so I could find my own way out.

That's what freedom is, finding out who you are, what works for you, and using all the help you need to find your own way out. If your experience is similar to mine, you will discover that your path will be different from that of your friends who are on this same journey. Our destination is the same. That destination is the ability to tell the TRUTH about ourselves.

There are two very definite reasons why for years and years I wanted no part of the truth. One, I believed I was "fundamentally bad, inadequate, defective, unworthy, and not fully valid as a human being." Two, on an intuitive level, I knew truth meant pain. I was still operating with my survival rules from childhood and believed that feeling pain was bad and meant something was wrong with me.

Getting down to the core of you – who you really are – is achieved by peeling off one painful layer of oppression at a time.

Today I know pain is the doorway to freedom. I'm not necessarily thrilled with that reality, but it's the truth. And I have found it to be true with all of the people I have talked to and worked with on the family of origin.

Many books written for adult children of alcoholics and co-dependents have a tendency to make it sound as if the recovery process, doing the family-of-origin work, is a clean, neat, brief, tidy little process. I have no idea why they do that; it confused the hell out of me.

My major issue, one that I still haven't gotten completely

free from, is the belief that deep down there is something terribly wrong with me. When I would be in the middle of peeling off a painful layer of oppression, it went something like this. I cried, snot running from my nose, and sobbed so hard that it felt like someone inside was trying to kick his way to freedom. My chest felt as though it was going to explode from holding my breath in an attempt to stuff the feelings. My muscles tied in knots from trying to hang onto the feelings. My throat ached from trying to strangle off the screams and at the same time was burned raw from screaming, and my knuckles would bleed from beating on the couch in my therapist's office. Sooo, when I would go home and read a book that made the process sound neat, brief, clean, and tidy – guess how I felt? Right! Like I was "fundamentally bad, inadequate, defective, unworthy, and not fully valid as a human being."

I would always take the book I had read and the feeling of not being okay to my therapist. She would lovingly reassure me that I was in MY place in the process, doing the work I had to do, at the level I had to do it. She would go on to remind me that others were in their place in the process doing the work they had to do at the level they had to do it. And that I was just fine.

There is some valuable information in the books. The point I'm trying to make is that we place too much importance on authority figures. We're used to taking something we overhear a knowledgeable looking person say and making it part of our belief system for the rest of our lives. We never stop to think that the guy may have just been released from the local ashtray factory. So if some of the formulas, answers, input in the books you read or have read confuses you or makes crazy – IT DOESN'T MEAN THERE IS ANYTHING WRONG WITH YOU!! It may mean the author has struck some old pain that you have buried. Or it may mean your experience is different from the author's. It could even mean that the author hasn't gone to the depths that you have on his or her own family-of-origin work. There are a number of people who have all this family-of-origin material stored in their heads, but they haven't let themselves feel the feelings.

Every minute of my family-of-origin work wasn't like I just described. There was a lot of awareness work leading up to each layer of oppression and repression. Some of the awareness work was even fun, because I learned that my childhood survival belief system no longer applied today and was able to laugh at myself. Then after peeling off a layer I would feel lighter, sometimes giddy, more okay than I had ever felt in my life – as though I was worth taking care of.

For those of you who are dismayed by all this, I want you to know you can do neat, clean, tidy, and brief family-of-origin work. And you will get exactly what it sounds like you will get – neat, clean, tidy, and brief results.

This kind of superficial work has real appeal. I can remember times when I would be on a break between peeling off layers, and I would walk into my therapist's office telling her how I had to get to the studio right after the session and finish a rush script. So, I didn't have the time or energy to get into anything heavy. I was still operating under the belief that the open expression of feelings was exhausting. Anyway, she would take me through some gut-wrenching, sobbing, couch-pounding incident, pat me on the butt, and send me off to the studio, where I would do more work and better work than I had ever done. The TRUTH is, suppressing or repressing feelings is exhausting. Expressing feelings is energizing.

I had to use an amount of energy equal to that of the feelings I was trying to express. The expenditure of that energy had become second nature to me. It wasn't something I was conscious of. I was just tired all the time. Of course I couldn't let anyone know I was tired all the time because that would have meant something was wrong with me. After I quit taking speed (amphetamines) by the barrel, I turned to consuming swimming pools of coffee, dump trucks full of sugar, and thousands of cubic feet of tar and nicotine to keep going.

Giving up all or any of alcohol, drugs, caffeine, sugar, or nicotine is a great way to start pulling some nails out of the coffin lid you've got covering your feelings.

In doing the family-of-origin work most of us will encounter all three of the angel/demons: repression, suppression, and splitting off. They are angels when we are children because they protect us from the pain that's too painful to live with. They are demons when we are adults because they keep us in prison.

When I began my family-of-origin work, I was one of the ones who couldn't remember more than a couple incidents form birth to age fifteen. *Repression:* burying the truth so deep in the unconscious mind that it can't be found without a concentrated effort. And even then some of it will remain in the mental graveyard forever.

On the other hand, my best friend Tom is one of those who finally woke up one day and realized he had been mourning the loss of a childhood that never existed. *Suppression:* shoving the truth down just far enough to cover it up with wishful, pain-free, anger-free, conflict-free thinking. Easier to get to but no less painful when found.

Splitting off: children split off (emotionally leave their body and go across the room) when what is happening is so painful, so frightening that they believe they or a member of the family is about to die. Adults who split off as children can recall and relate horrible truths from their childhood without the slightest sign of emotion. That's because, for them, it's like watching somebody that looks like them on a movie screen. Freedom for them is the same as for the rest of us. It comes when the feelings are connected with the truth, expressed and experienced for the first time.

I made a gargantuan effort to get to freedom by skipping the pain and going straight to God. I tried countless forms of meditation and numerous metaphysical philosophies. I worked hard at them, sometimes hours every day for months. Occasionally, the inner stirrings would stop for minutes, sometimes even days. But back the stirrings would come, even stronger than before.

I realize now that my attempts at meditation were no more than disguised suppression, repression, and splitting off. Trying to meditate was one more way to cut me off from my feelings. I still don't have any trouble leaving. My problem is being here, now.

John James says, "When it comes to grief, the phrase 'turn it over' is an avoidance phrase: one more way of not dealing with pain that needs to be dealt with in order to get free, one more way of avoiding saying goodbye to the old, which must be done before you say hello to the new." I agree wholeheartedly and would like to add that I think it's an avoidance phrase where most things are concerned.

What works for me (and it took me a long time and a lot of family-of-origin work to learn) is that when a situation comes up, first I try to get in touch with my feelings, then honor my feelings, then express my feelings. After I've done that, I can take whatever action is required – which at that point may be "turning it over."

A caution here: some days, I just had to avoid the trauma of trying to confront my feelings. I believed at the time that it would have been too painful. But I learned that just because I had to avoid something one day, didn't mean I had to try to avoid it for the rest of my life. Maybe one week I couldn't do any family-of-origin work. But the next week or the week after, I'd be back at it. Other times I would just have to stop my rush for perfect mental health and take time to stop and smell the flowers.

Each person has to go at his or her own pace! Some people attack these issues like the hare, others more like the tortoise. There is no right or wrong when it comes to doing the family-of-origin work. There is only what works for you. I am suspicious of people and workshops or seminars that want to rush people through this process. As my friend Tom Alibrandi says, "If anybody tells you that his way is the only way – grab your wallet and run for the door."

Find one or two people who are trying to work on these issues and are going about the same pace you are. Hang out together and try and give each other a hand.

CHAPTER 3

Animal, Vegetable, or Mineral?

My belief system tells me that to experience and express feelings is weakness. The tragedy contained in that lie is of monstrous proportions.

The TRUTH is that I AM MY FEELINGS, they are God given and meant to be experienced and expressed. The fact that I feel differently than the next person about something is my uniqueness. It's who I am.

Because we can't honor our feelings, the death march of the co-dependent goes something like this – we eat food we don't want to eat, we go to movies and other places we don't want to go to, we live in houses, neighborhoods, cities, states, countries we don't want to live in; we're in relationships that are abusive, empty, controlling, and oppressive; we make love when we don't want to make love. The march goes on and on and on.

I arrived at the conclusion that I am my feelings by figuring out all the things I am not. I am not my house because if it were destroyed tonight, I'd still be here. I am not my car because if it were stolen I'd still be here. I am not my job because if I lost or left it, I'd still be here. I'm am not my money or absence of it because one letter from the IRS or the Publishers Sweepstakes would reverse my fortunes, and I'd still be here. I am not my relationship because if it ended, I'd still be here. I am not my body because even as it changes, I'll still be here. I am not my personality because it can change from room to room at a party. What am I then if I am not my feelings?

My wife Tina and I are proud, frightened, excited, nervous, imperfect parents of a five-month-old baby daughter. I assure you that she arrived on this planet with a full set of feelings and the ability to express them, along with the ability to make her needs known to others.

I believe God gave every one of us a full package of feelings. I believe God fully intended that we honor and respect these feelings in ourselves and others. I believe God intended that we experience and express the feelings. I believe that's why some people call the oppression of a child's true nature "soul death." I believe that twelve-step recovery (Alcoholics Anonymous or any similar program), individual therapy, group therapy, body work, rebirthing, scream therapy, breathing therapy, grief work, yoga, exercise, nutrition, and so forth, are tools provided by God to enable us to get in touch with our feelings and get back to being what God originally intended us to be in the first place: happy, joyous, and free!

Yes, most of the above can also be used to keep your feelings frozen. But, if that's the place you're in – you know it.

I can hear some of you out there screaming "we are not our feelings – we are spirit!"

I made many serious attempts to leave my race consciousness behind and soar like an eagle. *Race consciousness* is a metaphysical term the now dead, modern day prophet Joel Goldsmith used to describe being HERE, NOW, on human level.

My problem with soaring like an eagle came as a result of a faulty navigational system that had been prepared for me by my parents. I kept flying into the sides of buildings from my past.

I don't believe I can soar with the spirits until I can first let myself be a human being, which means that whole catastrophe of experiencing feelings coupled with the knowledge that "Shit Happens" on this level, whether I'm soaring in the clouds or have my feet firmly planted on earth.

The desire to soar was coupled with the desire to be a spiritually perfect person: a spiritual giant among men, a person who, like many I have met, walks through life unruffled, chanting, ooommming, and feeling nothing.

What I've learned is that prayer and meditation misused are effective tools in accomplishing the suppression or repression of feelings. And repression is repression is repression, no matter how socially acceptable my method of achieving it. On the occasions I was able to still my inner stirrings and quiet the crying out of my inner child, my body was walking around, but let me assure you, nobody was home; in other words I was like an inanimate substance, a mineral. I was out there moving around but nothing affected me. And I was moving in a circle of friends at the time where that condition received praise.

I was so successful for a while at being a spiritual giant that when a wife I loved very much died, I held my head high and marched around waving the "God Took Her Home" banner. The grief and feelings I needed to experience were neatly and deeply stuffed. It would be ten years after her death before I was able to experience my feelings over the loss.

Another method I had for shutting down was to take up residence in front of the TV set. As a TV writer, I could always use the excuse that I was studying possible shows to write for. I just sat and stared – in other words, vegetated.

I hunted down and embraced any distraction that kept me from having to experience my feelings, from the truth of what happened to me, and from sharing with others the truth about me.

Freedom comes when I can share with others the truth

about me, something I must do whether I'm giving workshops, talking at a college, or with my wife in the safety of our home.

The words safety and home were anything but synonymous for me for most of my life, including my parents' home and homes that I created for myself and others. Today that has changed. Home and safe come to mind at the same time.

I believe that the intuition of my inner child is undamaged. His instincts are a little screwed up, but his intuition is perfect. I believe that God speaks to me through this inner child's intuition.

Looking back over my life, including the period when I was addicted to drugs and alcohol, I can recall numerous times the small voice (my intuition) would speak to me. "I don't think we should do this. This is not one of your better ideas," it would say. Only I couldn't honor it. I couldn't trust my intuition and not go ahead with whatever the plan was. I was making my decisions based on fear, a need to control, fear of abandonment, a sense of being less than, a need to look good, a need to keep the peace, a need to make people like me. I would talk myself out of the wisdom of my intuition and march straight ahead where I would find myself in Dante's Inferno, comfortable and familiar but still Dante's Inferno. Or the small voice would say "I think we should go there." What the voice was suggesting would be something I knew I wasn't prepared for. It would probably require risk and change. The possibility of risk and change frightened me. I knew for an absolute certainty that the moment I got off familiar ground, out of my element, people would discover my secret. They would find out that there was something wrong with me. So I wouldn't go. Later I would discover the people who went ahead and took the risk had found the pearl in the oyster.

Risk and change are the most common road signs on the path my intuition chooses to follow.

When I am experiencing (in touch with) my FEELINGS, when I am expressing my FEELINGS, I am whole. My car, job, house, wife, daughter, and friends don't make me whole.

Without my feelings I am incomplete. I don't exist. With my feelings I am whole.

When I am whole, I believe then I am what God intended me to be.

And when I am whole, I am able to follow the path my intuition lays out for me. Sure, risk and change can still scare me. But the difference is I can go ahead anyway. I don't have to talk myself out of going and miss the pearl God has put in the oyster.

The pearl may turn out to be a painful experience that forces me to peel off another layer of oppression. Or it may turn out to be a joyful experience that I find I can't let myself enjoy, which forces me to peel off another layer of oppression. But the act of peeling moves me closer to me, closer to my God, closer to freedom.

If God didn't intend for me to experience life here on the animal/human level – then why did he put me here?

CHAPTER 4

Hi There!

I never really knew I had an inner child. Oh sure, the child would cry out to me, but his voice was soft, hard to hear. Besides, I had thirteen other voices (the committee) in my mind, chattering and screaming from the time I got up until I went to sleep at night. The voices could never agree on anything, which meant they never stopped talking. I would get so tired of listening I just wanted to unscrew my head, leave it alongside the road, and drive off. I've noticed that when people pick up a gun to kill themselves, they don't as a rule shoot themselves in the stomach or the foot. They shoot themselves in the head, which, I'm convinced, is to stop the voices.

For years I shut up the voices with drugs and alcohol. When I stopped using the drugs and alcohol, they started up again. After the first couple of years of their renewed on-slaught, I began to get the sense that they were pulling me away from something, that they were tearing me apart. But I didn't know the who, why, what, when, or where of what was going on. And when the inner child would try and make his presence known, one of the committee would scream, "It's something you ate – take some Rolaids."

I have since learned that the committee is compulsive thinking, another way to separate myself from my feelings, my inner child.

The method I use to get out of my head into my feelings is to do some deep breathing. Then, I try and make myself pay attention to my body – to notice if my back hurts, or my neck is stiff, or my eyes are tired. I notice whether I'm sitting or standing. The first few years I learned to do that, it was a very scary experience. I would start to ease out of my head, and it was like being in the front seat of the front car on the roller coaster as it crept up to the top of the first big drop. Every part of me with exception of the inner child was scream-ing, "No! No! No! Don't go." The kid was yelling, "Yahoo, let's do it!"

Sometimes it's still like the big roller coaster drop, but to-day I know nothing bad is going to happen to me, so I try and join the kid in shouting, "Yahoo!"

One of the reasons it was so scary coming out of my head into my feelings was how I felt. I felt raw – vulnerable and raw, like the protective layer of my skin had been peeled off. In a way it had. All of the internal armor (walls) I had built to protect myself was starting to crumble, and it was fright-ening. I interpreted all feelings as bad or wrong. What I didn't understand was that I was feeling life for the very first time since earliest childhood.

My first conscious encounter with my inner child came during my first or second session with my therapist. She took me on a fantasy walk down a country road.

She explained to me that I was walking down this road alone. She described for me the dirt road, the fields on one side of the road, and the hills and trees on the other side. Then she told me to look up the road and see a huge tree. The kind of tree where half the roots are above ground and form benches for people and canyons for elves. Once I could see the tree, she told me to see a small figure sitting on top of one of the roots. As I got closer to the tree, she told me that I could see it was a small boy. As I got closer still, she told me I could see that the boy was me as a child. When I was standing right in front of the seated little Bobby, she asked me to tell her his age. I told her about three or four.

It was strange seeing myself as a boy sitting on that root. But there was no doubt in my mind that the three-year-old boy leaning slightly away from me was me. I was confused and uncomfortable. I had no idea what to say to the boy or what to do with him. And he didn't seem anxious to start anything up.

Margie told me to ask the boy if he'd like to go for a walk with me. I extended my hand and said, "Would you like to go for walk with me? What happened next made me very sad. He pulled back even further; the expression on his face was one of fear and distrust. He didn't want to go with me.

I told Margie he didn't want to go. She had me tell him that I would take good care of him, and he would be safe. So I said to the boy, "It'll be okay. I'll take good care of you. You'll be safe." The second I uttered those words something inside of me went soft. I didn't know what went soft. I didn't know why it went soft. I just knew that for the first time since I could remember, I felt like there was more to me than just "bad, inadequate, defective, unworthy, or not fully valid as a human being." The minute I offered to take care of little Bobby, I no longer felt so ashamed of myself.

Reluctantly, he took my hand.

We started off down the road. He walked on my right side – on the side of the fields. He walked leaning ever so slightly away from me. He walked slowly. I slowed my pace to match his, and the moment I did, I remembered being dragged along by my parents much faster than my little feet or feelings were able to go.

We traveled down the road for a while at his pace. He relaxed his arm and moved in a little closer. I felt my heart smile. Margie then told me to see a man coming over a rise in the road. He was headed straight for us. She told me the man was my father (who had been dead for fifteen years).

The last time I saw my father alive was when I was eighteen years old. I was embracing my alcoholism and drug addiction, and he was being strangled by his. He and my mother had been divorced for four years. He hadn't written or sent a nickel of child support. My last words to him were, "Why don't you go fuck off and die!"

When I was twenty-seven years old and had been off the drugs and alcohol for six months, I started to try to find my father. I wanted to tell him there was a way out. He died a year later, before I could find him.

My father stopped in the road in front of us. I said, "Hi." He said nothing. He just sort of stared straight ahead not seeing me or the boy. I told him to say hi to the boy. He kept staring off into nothingness.

Little Bobby was looking up at this man. He was anxiously waiting for recognition. His face was expectant, hopeful. Finally, little Bobby shuffled his feet in an attempt to draw attention to himself. My father just stared straight ahead. Again I asked my father to say hi to little Bobby. He continued to ignore the child. I screamed at him to look at the little boy. He wouldn't or couldn't.

I reached out and grabbed my father's hair and tried to bend his head down in an attempt to force him to see the child. He stiffened his neck. I yanked with all of my might to get him to bend his head. He wouldn't look. Although I had succeeded in bending his head down, he just looked off to his left. He refused to acknowledge the presence of me or the child. I began to understand where I learned to ignore me, ignore the child, ignore my needs, ignore my feelings.

I was angry, enraged, homicidal. I yelled at him that among other things he was a rotten, no good son of a bitch, and I'd like to kill him. His expression never changed. He kept staring off into nothingness – into that place in space where he was protected from his feelings.

Margie had me release him. I released him. She instructed little Bobby and me to say goodbye to him. We did, and without saying a word, he turned and started back in the direction he came from. Little Bobby and I called out one more goodbye and waved. Maybe just maybe. No. Not this time. Not ever. The man whose love, attention, and approval we had never been able to get disappeared over the hill without ever looking back. Inside, I felt empty and abandoned. A cold chill settled in, followed by sadness. I looked down at little Bobby. He looked straight into my eyes, and I realized we were feeling identical feelings. We were connected.

Margie told me to take little Bobby and continue down the road.

I took his hand. He didn't lean away this time. We continued on. We were walking more slowly than we had been before we stopped. It was as if we didn't want to risk catching up to the man who had just gone over the hill in front of us.

After we traveled over the top of the hill and there was no sign of my father, little Bobby picked up the pace.

It wasn't much farther before we came to a long dirt drive. Up at the end of the drive was a house. Little Bobby stopped. He wanted to go see the house. I didn't know what to do. Margie encouraged me to take the child to see the house. As I moved up the dirt drive with little Bobby, I realized the only "Keep Out" and "No Trespassing" signs were in my head.

As we got close to the house, I could see that one-half of the house was very nice. It was neat and clean with fresh paint, all the gingerbread was intact, pretty curtains showed through the windows, and there was well-maintained furniture on the porch. The other half was weathered, unpainted, had broken windows and pieces missing from the gingerbread, and no porch furniture.

We walked around the house. It was the same in back as in front. Once back around front, little Bobby let go of my hand and jumped up on the porch. I wanted to stop him. I was afraid somebody would come out of the house and yell at us, embarrass me. Nothing happened. He wanted to go in the house. Again, I didn't know what to do. My choice would have been to leave. I didn't like going places where I didn't know what to expect (the need for control and the fear of looking foolish).

At Margie's urging, little Bobby and I entered the house.

The inside was identical to the outside: half was neat, tidy, beautiful but cold, no personality; the other half was dirty, dusty, had cobwebs, and was falling apart. Little Bobby wandered around inside checking things out. After a few moments, he was ready to go. As we exited the house and walked down the drive, I realized, with Margie's help, that the child was just curious. He didn't want anything, didn't expect anything. I didn't understand because early on as a child my curiosity was smashed. You were seen, not heard, and you sure as hell didn't go around checking things out.

Once we were back out on the road, Margie had us return to the tree. Then, as we stood under the tree, Margie told me to pick little Bobby up and place him inside of me. I picked him up and just as I started to shove him into me feet first, stomach high, he began to kick and cry. He didn't want to go. He was afraid. Margie instructed me to ask him what was wrong. I did. He told me he didn't trust me. He expected me to keep him a prisoner like my parents had. He liked being out. He didn't want to go back. At Margie's urging, I told little Bobby I would do my very best not to make him a prisoner like my parents had. He liked being out. He didn't want to go back. At Margie's urging, I told little Bobby I would do my very best not to make him a prisoner ever again, and that it would mean so much to me if he would get inside for now. He relented and let me slip him inside, but he was frightened and unwilling.

I told Margie that I was touched that little Bobby trusted me enough to show me his curiosity and very surprised he was coming home with me. She explained to me that no matter how frightened and resistant little Bobby might be – I was all he had. I was his only hope. Without me, he would remain a prisoner forever. And without him, I would remain a prisoner forever.

She asked me what I thought about the house that little Bobby and I had visited on the walk.

I told her the house was a perfect example of a chemically dependent home: half of it was falling apart, and the other half was keeping up appearances, and that was exactly what I was currently doing with my life. I was falling apart on the inside and using all of my resources to keep it from showing on the outside.

Margie sent little Bobby and me home to begin the adventure.

Today, instead of *acting as if*, I try hard to honor little Bobby's wishes and show *what it is*.

Jesus said "You must become as little children to enter the kingdom of heaven." There are metaphysical teachers and prophets who will tell you it is through the inner child that God speaks to you. Others say the inner child is God. In *Models of Love*, Joyce and Barry Vissell quote Rabbi Schlomo Carlebach: "Many have come to teach the holiness of God, but still there is not peace in the world. Many have come to teach the holiness of man, and still there is not peace in the world. When many come to teach the holiness of children, then there will be peace in the world."

If you are going to begin or have already begun this trek back into the wild, terrifying jungle called your family of origin, I think it is critical that you learn the holiness of your inner child, that little person who has been hiding in fear for so long. I have learned the hard way that the only way I am able to see the holiness of others is to experience my own holiness.

Young children who themselves are being loved and nurtured will not let another child go hungry, go without a place to stay, or be beaten or hurt without telling someone. So maybe, just maybe, when we honor the holiness of our young inner child, the hungry will be fed, the homeless will be housed, the abuse of women and children will stop, and there will be peace – not just peace in our homes, in our neighborhoods, in our cities – but peace in the world.

CHAPTER 5

"No Big Deal"

Minimization is the bastard child of the demon/angels –
repression, suppression, and splitting off.

According to the *New World Dictionary:* Minimize 1. to
reduce to a minimum; decrease to the least possible amount,
degree, etc. 2. to estimate or make appear to be of the least
possible amount, value, or importance.

Once little Bobby and I had been launched out into the
world by Margie, I spend most of the first two or three years
trying to convince myself and little Bobby that what had happened to us in the past or what was happening to us at the
moment was "no big deal," my way of continuing to decrease
my feelings to the least possible amount.

It wasn't difficult for me. I'd been doing it all of my life.
Hardly a day would go by that I wasn't telling myself and
others, "I don't care;" "It's not important;" "It doesn't matter;"
"It's okay, don't worry about it;" "I'm fine;" "No big deal;" "I'm
trying to live in the moment;" "God's will;" "There are no big
deals."

Most of that behavior was learned in childhood. Almost everything was diminished, my feelings, my losses, my desires, my dreams, my attempts, my life – "You're lucky to have a couch to sleep on, plenty of kids don't even have that."

We didn't have much money when I was a child, so at Christmas I would take three or four kitchen utensils and wrap them up, and that way I would have presents for my mother. On Christmas Day she would unwrap them and give me hell for wasting wrapping paper.

I remember giving my dad a rock once. I found it playing soldier in a vacant lot. I washed it with the hose at the gas station. I polished it on my pants. He threw it away. It was just a rock.

Today if my inner child picks up rocks when I'm hiking, I pocket them all and take them home. We put them on a dresser or nightstand in a place of honor; there they stay until the inner child and I agree on the rocks' next resting place.

We lived upstairs over a cosmetics factory, and on more than one occasion I spent an entire afternoon digging through the fifty-five-gallon drum trash cans in order to put together a compact for my mother. I would find the best compact with the smallest crack, a mirror that wasn't broken, a clean puff, and a clean unbroken pad of makeup. Proud as could be, I would take my find upstairs to Mom. It would be thrown away.

In grammar school I would draw a picture, but it wasn't as good as the other kids'. I wanted to draw a different picture, but I was already too afraid to rock the boat. At Cub Scouts I would make a plaque or pot holder, but it wasn't as good as the other ones. I wanted to make a different plaque and different pot holder, but was afraid to rock the boat. It was always put in the "not as good as" category.

My mother would give the things I made in Cub Scouts a place of honor in the house – for a week. Then they would disappear.

It only took so much, then I got the message. What I did, thought, or felt wasn't "as good as," wasn't important.

Many of the professionals say our society is dysfunctional,

co-dependent. One look at the school system supports that. First you have the grading system, which is the educators' means of control. Pass-fail also confirms what the children are being told at home: "You're stupid, you're not as good as, your ideas stink, you're not important." Or, conversely, the family hero is being told that he or she is important and wonderful because of his or her performance. I cringe every time I see a bumper sticker announcing "I'M PROUD – MY CHILD IS AN HONOR STUDENT AT POEDUNK SCHOOL." Where are the bumper stickers that say "I'M PROUD OF MY CHILD." To use success in the classroom as a yardstick of a child's worth is a brutal and abusive concept.

I never finished high school. The threw me out in the tenth grade. They told my mother to get me a job. I was too difficult for the school system. I usually got unsatisfactory in just about everything. With the exception of my sixth grade teacher, I was bored, bored, bored. I cut school every chance I got. What was going on in the world was a hell of a lot more interesting than what was going on in school. Also, when I was wandering around in the world, the shame wasn't as terrible as it was in school. I failed English ever since the fourth grade. I used to be a phonetic speller. My spelling has improved from writing things that interest me, excite me, entertain me and others. In the last twenty years as a writer, I have made over a million dollars. Of course, as a direct result of the issues I am writing about in this book, I managed to throw it all, and I mean all, away.

Most of the information people learned in order to graduate from high school has very little to do with what's required of them on the job. The important aspect of the high school diploma is the acknowledgment from one dysfunctional system to another that the bearer can be controlled.

I and others exercise control over me by minimizing my feelings, dreams, efforts, needs, accomplishments, and my past and by attaching my acceptance to my ability to conform.

The danger of minimizing is that I never get to how I REALLY FEEL. I don't know how I really feel, I don't know who I am or what I need.

Now to some of you, statements like "being dragged along by my parents much faster than my little feet or feelings could go" or "as a child my curiosity was smashed," or "he threw the rock away," may sound like I'm blaming my parents. At the time, I was. While I was taking the fantasy walk and early into discovering the truth about my childhood, I wasn't able to connect that my parents had probably been dragged along by their parents faster than their little feet and feelings could go.

I learned it was harmful for me to make the connection between what was done to me and what was done to my parents while I was in the process of uncovering incidents from the past for the first time. On the occasions I did, it only served to diminish the anger or sadness I felt, and consequently, it took longer and made it harder for me to peel off that layer of oppression. When I didn't allow myself (my child) to express the full force, depth, and range of my (our) anger, all I did was put an old, dirty bandage on an open wound.

I was minimizing, telling myself that I shouldn't be so upset. They did the best they could with the tools they had. Or I would try a little suppression by recalling the incident through rose-colored glasses, trying to make reality what I wanted it to be rather than what it was. I still do that. I'll take the aisle seat on an airplane and somehow convince myself that I'm not thirty-five thousand feet above the ground. Or I won't look in the rearview mirror when speeding, the logic being, if I don't look, there is no policeman. If I don't look, there is no me.

When I was ready to start forgiving my parents, the attitude that "they did the best they could with the tools they had" was a blessing. But until I WAS READY, that attitude was like a bucket of cold water being thrown in my face. I would immediately cool down emotionally, even though I was in the middle of a memory of a beating, withheld love, conditional love, verbal abuse, sexual abuse, emotional abandonment, or physical abandonment.

The one thing I didn't need initially was to be understanding. I needed to get so mad I'd beat pillows and couches until my knuckles bled, or I needed to scream underwater or into pillows until my throat was raw, or I needed to sob and cry until my physical hurt eased the emotional hurt. Being understanding at the expense of my feelings is a form of minimizing, a form of selling me out one more time. When forced to, I would acknowledge to others that an incident had in fact taken place, but not acknowledge that the incident had any impact on me.

The original abandonment issue is between me and my parents. The MAJOR abandonment issue is between ME AND ME – between me and the inner child. This abandonment of myself began as a child in order to get along, survive, stop the pain. As an adult I continued to do it to stop the pain, to get along, to survive, and because it was all I knew how to do. The tools required for the job in adulthood are the same tools required in childhood: repressing, suppressing, oppressing, splitting off, and minimizing.

My body would signal me that it need to go to the bathroom. I would respond by telling myself that it wasn't that bad, it could wait until later. Then I'd put it off until I physically hurt. I still do that one.

When I was in a group of people who were trying to decide where to go for dinner, the movies, or some other form of entertainment, I usually had no input because I didn't allow myself to get in touch with how much I'd like to go to a specific place. On the off chance I did suggest some place, it was designed to impress them – somewhere I had been before and didn't feel entirely like a fish out of water. It didn't have anything to do with what I liked. I probably didn't know what I liked. Occasionally, if I was in a group where I felt superior or stronger, I'd still pick a place where I knew I would be comfortable and where I thought they would be impressed.

Externally I never let anyone know if I was really looking forward to something. The reason? I didn't let me know I was looking forward to it. I was raised in a constant state of disappointment. And, if I verbalized my disappointment (at ages three, four, and five), I was made to feel there was something wrong with me. So not looking forward to things was learned behavior. Survival behavior – as an adult, it's just one more bar in the prison window.

One of the ways I split off doing the family-of-origin work is to say things like "my mother beat the hell out of him" or "my dad didn't love him." It effectively removed me from the feelings. I, on occasion, will still do that. Some days I just don't want to feel the feelings. And for those moments I choose to split off, I cease to exist.

Once the relationship started to grow between me and little Bobby, he was quick to suggest things to do and places to go. Sadly, most of the time, I would have to talk him out of it. I would minimize the importance of what he wanted to do. I wasn't ready to try new adventures. I was still worried about looking good. I was worried that people would see that I didn't know how to do something. I wasn't ready for risk and spontaneity. I need emotionally and image-safe choices. I was still quite capable of selling me out.

I never minded changing a television script I had written. My work and the characters I had created weren't important. I knew my being a writer was a fluke, that someday "they" would find me out. They would find out I was "fundamentally bad, inadequate, defective, unworthy, or not fully valid as a human being," and I'd be finished.

I never minded giving in on almost all points in a relationship. I knew they would eventually find me out. I would just mark time and put off the inevitable as long as I could.

The list, of course, goes on and on. But what happened is, the longer I did my family-of-origin work and the more I got in touch with my feelings, it suddenly started to hurt to change my characters, to give in. Initially to stop the hurt, I started to stand up for myself. Today, I stand up for myself because it feels good. I try hard today not to suppress, minimize, or split off. I still do all three, but usually I'm aware of it.

When I split off, I become this robot trying to be all things to all people. I completely lose touch with my body and its needs. I lose touch with myself and my emotional needs. If my wife is unable to get me to see that I have disconnected from myself, my body lets me know by getting sick.

When I catch myself trying to suppress something, I can laugh. On more than one occasion my attempts to suppress have been called to my attention by flashing red lights in the rearview mirror.

Often when I start to minimize, I have this sense of a soft sell used-car salesman inside of me trying to sell me some pain-free, second-hand emotions. If I refuse to sign the contract, Mr. Soft Sell turns me over to the grinder, the hard-sell, high-pressure man. Some days I don't get out without signing the contract. Most days I do.

CHAPTER 6

"Hitting the Streets"

It was tough and unpleasant getting in touch with feelings in the safety of Margie's office. It was also a little bit wonderful. But when I hit the streets with some of my new-found information, I found out what tough and unpleasant really meant. But, it, too, was also a little bit wonderful.

I have always felt that people who are newly graduated from an assertiveness training course should be made to wear a banner across their chest announcing the accomplishment, so that the poor waiters, waitresses, store clerks, gas station attendants, mates, and friends who catch the initial volley of gunfire will know why. People who have never been assertive in their lives don't know at the core of their being that it's okay to stand up for themselves. An assertiveness training course doesn't change that, it only convinces them on an intellectual level. Not believing they have a right to stand up for themselves on an emotional level, they approach their initial test runs from a defensive posture. They attack rather than assert.

I am now equally convinced there should be a handbook and banner for the people just getting in touch with or just learning to express their feelings.

Little children living in a functional home who are in the process of getting in touch with their feelings do so in a supportive environment. Those of us who have to start this process all over again as adults aren't as lucky.

Once I started getting in touch with my feelings and needs, it seemed like everywhere I went was a mine field. Almost every encounter exploded in my face.

When I started to get in touch with some of my anger, I became aware of the suppressed and repressed anger of others. I would go to meetings of organizations I belonged to, and I could feel the suppressed and repressed anger buzzing in the room like an neon sign about to explode. I wanted to run away. I wanted to scream. I sat there like a good boy.

When I started to get in touch with some of my fear, awarness of the fear in others would send panic chills through me. I wanted to hide. I wanted to ask them what they were afraid of. I wanted to tell them I was afraid. I sat there like a good boy.

When I started to get in touch with some of my sadness, awareness of the repressed grief in others reached out, grabbed me by the throat, and strangled me so hard that the backs of my eyes burned. I wanted to cry. I wanted to ask them why they were so sad. I wanted to tell them that I was sad. I sat there like a good boy.

I didn't know how to say anything about what I was feeling. It was all so new to me. I was still operating under the belief that I had to look good. I didn't know how to express real feelings and look good. So the fear of looking foolish or being exposed, laughed at, yelled at, or abandoned kept me quiet.

I am one of those who, up until starting therapy, was completely out of touch with his feelings. Early experiences in therapy made my heart go out to those who were in touch with their feelings but unable to express them. What a horrible way to live. And to think it's learned survival behavior. Behavior that we still think will somehow protect us.

I am convinced that a large portion of disease and early deaths is caused by suppressed or repressed feelings. We rot inside one little piece at a time.

I didn't stay completely stuck in that place of not expressing identified feelings for long. It was too painful. It was a hundred times more painful than the tight ass, rigid, and controlled life I had been living. I knew I was going to have to start talking to people other than my therapist about what was going on with me.

The organization Adult Children of Alcoholics didn't exist at this time, and now that I was in touch with some feelings, I realized I didn't feel safe around any of the people I knew. I felt unsafe partly because I needed an excuse to avoid taking the risk of sharing feelings and partly because the hostility, fear, and denial in my friends was real.

A little bit at a time I started taking the risk of telling others the truth about myself, my feelings. It didn't turn out to be quite the happy, laughing, understanding, hugging, and sharing experience that I had hoped for.

The first person I decided to experiment on was the lady I was living with at the time. I told her I felt that every time she talked to me about anything she was attacking me, and her hostility made me afraid and angry.

She told me how hard it was living with someone who up until this point hadn't been in touch with any feelings, and it made her feel unloved and that frightened her and made her angry.

Wait a minute! I didn't want to know how she felt, that wasn't in my game plan. I wanted to tell her how I felt and let it drop. I wasn't prepared to hear her side. I had only gotten my head up high enough out of the swamp to speak the words. I was still chin deep in co-dependence issues. I felt responsible for how she felt. I felt that it was my duty to change it or fix it. I felt that at all costs I had to keep her from getting angry. I felt that somehow by talking about my feelings I had done something wrong; I had rocked the boat. A land mine had exploded in my face. If memory serves me, I just sulked off to the bedroom thinking about jumping from the balcony. That kind of thinking at that time could have had some serious consequences. We didn't live on the ground floor. It would not have been a simple headfirst dive into the bushes. We lived on the seventeenth floor.

The end result of my first attempt at expressing my feelings was that I wanted to kill myself. It would be a few weeks before I would try again. When the pain of avoiding expressing what I felt became too great, I tried again.

This time I picked a meeting of an organization I belong to. I told those present how I was just starting to get in touch with some of my suppressed and repressed anger. I went on to tell them about all the anger I felt in the room. Land mine number two went off. Everyone assured me they weren't angry. Some assured me that allowing myself to be angry could be very dangerous for me. According to them, anger was the dubious luxury of normal men. Others assured me that I wasn't angry, just confused. Still others wanted me to see that my feeling anger was an excellent example of the dangers of therapy.

Like a good co-dependent I had tried to prepare for this encounter before it took place. I had rehearsed my part and their parts. I went expecting a healthy discussion about anger. I went expecting people to express their feelings on the subject. Instead, I found myself in a room full of people who were trying to convince me that either I wasn't feeling what I was feeling or that if I did have a feeling, it was wrong. It took about two seconds for the old I am "fundamentally bad, inadequate, defective, unworthy, or not fully valid as a human being" to go off. I had been shamed.

This time I did not go quietly into the night. I waited until the meeting was over and then cornered a couple of people I knew better than the rest. Already tired of having land mines go off in my face, I attacked. I tried to make them see their anger. I tried to make them admit to the anger that had been in the room. The more I pushed them to look, the more they resisted. They minimized: "I may be upset a little, but it's no big deal." They looked to the heavens: "God is in charge; there is nothing to be angry about." They shamed me: "What is so wrong with you that you have to attack the people and organization that are saving your life?" Now I went quietly into the night. The same seventeenth-story balcony had renewed appeal.

Margie, my therapist, had been out of town during this three-week period. I was anxiously awaiting her return. I felt like a kid waiting for his fairy godmother to come flying through the window and fix everything with her magic wand.

I went into my session thinking anger was bad and that there was something wrong with me. She helped me see that anger is functional. That being in touch with my anger would show me where to start establishing boundaries and where to set some limits. If I get mad doing something for someone it may be an indicator that I don't want to be doing it in the first place.

She also helped me to understand that I'm not responsible for the feelings of others, and they are not responsible for mine. The bad news was that you only achieve knowledge by practice. Rehearsing at home alone wasn't going to do it. I was going to have to keep going out on the firing line and risking.

The adult was very resistant to go back out there into that mine field. But little Bobby, my inner child, was starting to get a tiny sense that we would be okay and that our freedom, his and mine, depended on our going forward.

Returning to the firing line, I noticed that I was changing. I no longer responded to every situation with frozen feelings. I wasn't as quick to drag up an old familiar personality in order to compensate for feeling ill at ease or out of place. I didn't always shut up rather than rock the boat. Don't misunderstand me; I was still fighting all the demons, just not as many and as often.

I found I was reluctant to say goodbye to the personalities that no longer served me. I believed that if I let go of one of these creations there would be nothing left but a void, a big nothing. Also, my wounded inner child felt that these old "friends" were still necessary for survival; they had kept him safe for years. The new information was that although they had kept him safe, they were destroying my life as an adult. Eventually, I decided to pretend that they never existed, that way I didn't have to feel the sadness.

I didn't really understand why there should be any sadness. I thought there was something wrong with me because I wasn't rejoicing. I didn't realize that saying goodbye to these old companions was the same as a death in the family. They had been part of life since I could remember. As I write this, I still haven't done all of the grieving work I need to to in order to say goodbye to that old gang of mine. They aren't great bedfellows when it comes to living, but they are definitely street smart when it comes to surviving.

One morning while I was shaving, I noticed the beginnings of a person looking back at me. I didn't know what to do with him, but there he was. The fact that I had never noticed him before made me sad. The next thing I noticed, of course, was that his ears weren't the same height. I immediately used that to confirm that I was flawed. I assumed all the other human beings on the planet had level ears. They don't.

Initially as I managed to claim my body I found fault with it. I remember enrolling in a Hatha Yoga class. The instructor kept the room at eighty-five degrees. Mirrors covered one wall. We worked out only in shorts – no shirts nor shoes. At this time I could still pinch a easy couple of inches of love handles (actually having gotten pregnant right along with my wife, I can again pinch an easy inch of love handles). I have one leg slightly shorter than the other, and my body has a tendency to lean to the right and my head to the left when I'm tired, a result of injuries when I was using drugs and drinking. We took a short break at the halfway point. I looked in the mirror at that perspiring mess and thought the kindest thing I could do would be to shoot him. Here I was taking a risk by trying something new, something that would benefit my health, and I couldn't give myself an ounce of praise. Thank God at the end of the class the instructor praised us for being there and for making a tremendous effort. As time went by, I was able to praise myself just for arriving at the class. And after the class, I would give the kid and me a treat for a job well done. We would go to a movie we really wanted to see or treat ourselves to a sugar-free snack.

I began to understand that in a functional setting there is room for more than one opinion. And even though there is more than one opinion, no one has to be wrong. I was raised in a home in which the only opinion was my father's; if he was at work, the only opinion was my mother's. I learned early on that opinions could get me hurt. I saw a great bumper sticker yesterday, "IT SHOULDN'T HURT TO BE A CHILD." I started to see that just because someone has a different opinion or different needs, it doesn't mean he is attacking the setting, the system, or me. I had spent my life obsessed with trying to make other people see it my way. If I ran into angry resistance, I gave in and saw it their way, quietly hating them for as long as I knew them.

WHEN I'M OKAY WITH ME, I HAVE NO NEED TO MAKE YOU WRONG.

I eventually noticed that the man in the mirror had eyes. Looking into the eyes, I saw the child. I realized my eyes were the mirror of my feelings, my child. My child had sad eyes. We had been apart for so long. I would try to convince the child that we wouldn't be apart again. He didn't believe me. He knew my capacity for splitting off from him, from myself. But I knew he was going to stick it out anyway. I didn't understand anybody sticking it out. My motto was "when the going gets tough, the tough leave."

So back out there I went, trying to learn how to live instead of how to survive. I told more people how I felt and would stand and listen while a couple of them told me how they felt. But I couldn't shake feeling that I was responsible for their feelings. I still felt I should fix their feelings or convince them that they didn't have them.

Soon I started to run into a situation that almost made me stop the whole process. It never dawned on me that my life was full of people and relatives who liked me as I had been. They were attached to the status quo. They didn't want changes in me, in my life, in themselves, or in their lives. When I started changing, they either dropped out of my life entirely or worked very hard at covert and overt ways of getting me back to the "old me."

They would come to me and tell me they were convinced that because of the stress of therapy I was going to drink or use drugs again. They would cite three or four unnamed people they supposedly knew who had done just that. I discovered later they had made up the unnamed examples in an attempt to validate their position. This is a major co-dependence issue. Things that I was doing to benefit or change me were viewed by others as a threat. This is common in couples, friends, acquaintances, and business associates. One person will begin to draw some limits and boundaries, and the other person will view it as the end. In order to stop what they perceive to be the end, they launch into a campaign to stop the person from changing.

People told me how terrible I looked. Neither they nor I knew that what they were saying was "You look different." They assumed because I looked different, it meant I looked terrible. Of course I looked different! The mask was starting to crumble. The real me was beginning to show through. A person was starting to emerge. The face was hatching from its protective shell and starting to show the feelings of the moment. People who knew me weren't used to that. They were accustomed to the poker face. The "everything is fine" face.

Some people attacked: "You used to be a nice guy, but lately you've become the most selfish son of a bitch I know." I had someone share with me at one of my workshops recently that when anyone accuses her of being selfish she explains to them that she is self-nurturing. I like that.

A major fallout began when I started saying NO to people who were accustomed to hearing yes from me. Guilt was one of their favorite weapons: "You used to do it." "I was counting on you." "You have to. There's nobody else." "You've always come for Christmas." "It's your responsibility to be there." "We need you." On the occasions when none of it worked, they disowned me or raged at me.

For a while it was tough. I felt like I was being hit with everything from Ping-Pong paddles to baseball bats by every person I met. I felt as if people were praying that I would self-destruct so that things would go back to "normal." But there was an intuitive drive that kept me going. As frightening as it felt, I was starting to taste freedom. I was starting to come alive. One plus I had going for me was the woman I lived with. Despite our differences, a couple of major fights, and our eventual breakup, she continued to encourage me to hang in there with my therapist. She was seeing her own therapist, doing her own changing, and knew the value. Besides, I think she was tired of hearing my voice change every time I got on the phone with my mother.

The first two or three years I was successful finding and expressing my feelings about one-quarter of the time. About one-eighth of the time, I was successful in expressing what I felt to others. The rest of the time was spent with frozen feelings, split off from myself or in that goddamn self-imposed exile of knowing what I felt and being afraid to verbalize it.

I had been afraid that I would never be able to remember enough about my childhood to get well. What I didn't realize was that the feelings I was discovering were the paths back to my repressed childhood memories. I would go to Margie with a feeling I had just discovered, and she would help me trace that feeling back through the dark forest of gremlins, goblins, witches, and trolls. I would get afraid in the dark forest. I would want to stop and not go on. I knew that soon I was going to have to experience sadness and anger, because eventually I would emerge from the forest and wind up right in the middle of those incidents in my childhood that had forced me to start repressng the very same feelings in the first place.

The more time I spent on the streets getting in touch with my feelings and the more time I spent with Margie tracing the feelings back, the more I began to understand who I was, how I was damaged, who did the damaging, and how it all dictated my current and past behavior. With that information in hand, I was starting to get a fix on what I could do to change it.

I could tell you the truth about me. Or as Carol MacHendrie, a therapist friend of mine in Santa Fe, describes intimacy, "Me being me and letting you see me."

CHAPTER 7

"Till My Past Do Us Part"

Using Carol's definition, I can safely say that intimacy was a rare commodity in my relationships.

I didn't know me so it was impossible to let anybody "see me." If anybody did "see me," it was because they had the ability to look past the problem, beyond the mask. If I showed myself to anybody, it was by mistake, and I deeply regretted it immediately afterwards.

My role models for relationships were the original dynamic duo, Mom and Dad. As far as I can piece it together, their relationship went something like this: Dad was thirty-six years old, had never been married, and was a functioning alcoholic. By functioning I mean that he went to work everyday, didn't wreck cars (didn't own one), and hadn't yet started to be unacceptably drunk in public. He was still operating within the "good time" range of social behavior. He had a secure job for an alcoholic. He was an auditor for the Government Accounting Office. He was tired of going home to an empty apartment. He was tired of living alone.

Mom was twenty-eight years old, had never been married, and was waiting for Sir Lancelot, even though she believed she wasn't worthy of a real honest-to-God Sir Lancelot. Her father had died when she was young. Her mother had died when she was eighteen, and she was left to raise her younger brother. Her younger brother was now out on his own. She had a good job with the power comapany in Golden, Colorado. Not only was she tired of going home to an empty apartment and tired of being alone, she was just plain tired.

They met. Dad knew he wasn't going to have to go home to an empty apartment any more. He wasn't going to be alone. Mom knew she had found her knight in shining armor who was going to take care of her. She too wasn't going to have an empty house anymore. She wasn't going to be alone.

I'm convinced that on some level Dad knew he had found the mother he had lost when he was a young boy. He had found a woman to take care of him.

Mom had taken care of her mother and her brother. Now she had somebody else who "needed" her.

They were both wrong about one thing though. In the next thirteen years, they were going to be more alone than they had ever been in their lives. My being born didn't change that for either one of them.

When I was eight years old we moved to California. My dad would go to work, come home, eat dinner, get drunk (his social behavior had started to slip), and go to bed. My mom would cook, clean, wash clothes, make excuses as to why my father ignored me, and go to bed. They rarely talked about anything. My mother would share newsy stuff about the relatives, and Dad would nod his head and keep eating or drinking. What I remember most from age eight on is silence, silence that in a few years would be interrupted by my being in trouble. In thirteen years maybe they went out six times. In the same thirteen years maybe we went out as a family six times. I grew up on the couch in the living room, which was straight across the hall from their bedroom door, and I can tell you something else they did maybe six times in thirteen years.

My mother divorced my dad when she became aware that at age twelve I was almost six feet tall and thinking about killing him. And she got tired of his leaving letters around the house from a female attorney in Salt Lake City with whom he was having an affair. I believe if it hadn't been for the letters, she would have stayed with him until somebody died.

There you have it. A brief thumbnail sketch of my introduction to relationships.

My first heartbreak came when I was fifteen, and my eighteen-year-old girlfriend slept with my best friend. Even though this was a crowd of people who drank, did drugs, and rebelled, her action confirmed for me what I had suspected: that I was "fundamentally bad, inadequate, defective, unworthy, or not fully valid as a human being." I knew that whatever I was, I wasn't good enough. My clothes weren't good enough, my car wasn't good enough, my drugs weren't good enough. But had you been present when that happened, you only would have heard me say, "Fuck that bitch, man, who needs her!" I had good masks already.

I started going to the pretend school for relationships. I dated mostly older girls and women. I was bound and determined to find out what they liked. Now before you start thinking "how thoughtful of him," let me make it perfectly clear that I only wanted to know so I could avoid a repeat of my first heartbreak. I didn't really care what they liked. I just wanted to avoid rejection and pain. I wanted to be able to seduce. I want to be held, kissed, and made love to. I wanted to be in control. And in order to accomplish those objectives, I was willing to pretend. What the hell, I didn't know what I liked or wanted or what love was. If I wasn't pretending, I was nothing. And with the conditioning I already had, there was more than just a little truth to that statement.

For classroom purposes I sought out the women who wanted me, the ones I viewed as easy. By the time I reached eighteen, I had my act underway, and I took the show out of town for tryouts. Actually, I was on the run from the law with some friends, and we wound up in Colorado.

I was now ready to try for some women who required a level of seducing I could deliver. And this is when I met my first wife.

I was working as an ambulance attendant for an ambulance company in Denver. One night we were hanging out in our quarters, and the dispatcher was on the telephone with a girl. As a joke, somebody took the phone away from him and started passing it around. When I got on the phone, my instinct said go for it. By the time I got off the phone, we had a date for later in the week.

When we met, she lived in a coeducational boarding house. I was drunk and two or three hours late for our first date. She didn't seem to mind. I had brought a bottle, and she proceeded to get drunk with me. We wound up the evening by having relaxed, drunken, uninhibited, first date sex.

It didn't take me long to convince her to move out of the boarding house into an apartment so we could have some on my time off. Shortly after she got the apartment, she became concerned about what her parents' reaction would be. She had the solution – marriage.

Wedding day rolled around, and although my instincts knew this was the perfect woman for me, my intuition, the still small voice, the inner child said to me, "I don't think this is a great idea." That was not going to be the last time that I was to hear those words in an identical setting.

Intuition is me, it's self, it's who I am. I didn't trust me or you. I knew all relationships were designed to end anyway. All the ones up close in my life had. I went by instinct. Instinct had all the survival tools. Instinct said that with this woman things will be okay, you'll be married, normal, like the rest of the people. I said I do.

The marriage turned into a stormy off again, on again situation covering the next six years of our lives. The union produced two daughters. I finally moved out. If I hadn't, she probably would have stayed until one of us died. Sound familiar?

I continued to drink and use drugs for six more months after I moved out. Then, finally, that specific dance of death was over.

Three weeks after I stopped using chemicals I met, as a friend of mine would say, my next future ex-wife.

She and I lived together for about a year when one night we went to a gathering in Laguna Beach. People there were ecstatic over their marriages to other nonusing addicted people. When we got back to the motel, she knew that what we needed to do was get married. Today, looking back, I believe on some level we both knew the relationship was over. We both knew that our time together had more than likely been the key ingredient in our being able to follow a program and stay off the chemicals. But we didn't know how to say goodbye. Neither of us had ever grieved over the loss of anything. We had stuffed everything. So, she said if we didn't get married, there would be no more sex.

At that point in my life that was one hell of an ultimatum. She was the only woman in my life with whom I had ever had sex, without the aid of chemicals. The thought of going out there into the world and trying to find someone else was frightening. I stayed up until four in the morning thinking. At four-thirty we loaded our stuff into the car and drove back to her place (where I was living). We packed up and hit the road for Las Vegas. One more time the instincts said to go for it, and the still small voice, the inner child, intuition said, "This is not a great idea." We got married.

Before we finally divorced two years later, we were separated and reunited more than six times.

I was always in control of the situation, of the other person, until I met resistance. Then I'd give in rather than risk further conflict. My concern over what others thought, coupled with my lack of self-esteem, caused me to sell out rather than risk a public scene. I'd give in rather than get the woman mad. I had a terrible fear of anger in a woman.

I realize now that by the time I was fifteen, most of my

feelings were already frozen. Those that weren't got dropped into the deep freeze when I had said, "Fuck that bitch, man, who needs her!"

With no feelngs, no sense of self, and no self-esteem, pretend school served me well. I put together what I call a vaudeville act. I had three songs and three dances that I used after the excitement of the initial seduction had worn off. I was to acquire a fourth dance after I became a writer.

The experience when I was fifteen taught me that for my peace of mind the first thing I needed to do in any new relationship was to eliminate the competition. I would accomplish this with bouquets of flowers, phone calls, cards professing undying love, singing telegrams, and weekends out of town. This flurry of activity was designed to build a fort around my intended subject. The fort was free from outside interference. I used to say that the fort was designed to keep them in, while I decided if I wanted them. I now know that the fort was designed to keep us both in while I made sure they wanted me.

This mating dance would begin when I spied an acceptable female. Because I had no sense of myself as a whole person (body, mind, feelings), it was impossible to see women as whole people. I viewed them in pieces: great legs, great ass, great breasts, beautiful face. My requirements were a sufficient blend of the above pieces to make me look good and to excite me. Now a great body alone wasn't enough. Whenever possible I wanted women who were better traveled and better educated. And it was imperative that they wanted me and had a look in their eyes that made sparks fly.

Once those requirements were met, I'd be off and running, building the fort.

Once the fort was built, the rush slowed down, some of the dust cleared, and we settled into the day-to-day routine of a relationship. Then the curtain call would come.

The curtain call was nothing more than my new partner needing an emotional fix. She needed to know that somebody occupied the body she had been eating with, sleeping with, and having sex with. More than likely she was sitting next to me and starting to feel very alone. At this moment she would appear to me like a small bird sitting in the nest with its beak wide open waiting for a worm. Not having any worms, I knew it was time to go into my vaudeville act and entertain. I would mount the stage, throw open the curtains, and sing my first song.

Now my first song would consist of taking said woman to the stereo system where I would play a song for her. I would tell her this was my favorite song – a song I worshipped in private, a song that made me cry every time I heard it – a song I had waited a long time to share with the right person. The song would bring tears to her eyes and to my eyes. We would hug and peace would reign again, for a while.

Before long, there she'd be in the nest again with beak wide open. Show time!

This time I would do a dance. I would load the love of my life in the car and drive her down to the beach, where after climbing over rocks, down the face of a cliff, and wading through the waves, we would come to rest in a small cove. I would explain that this cove was a sacred and special place to me. I would tell her how in the old days I would come to the cove alone to shoot morphine and be in peace. I'd tell her that since I stopped using drugs, I came to the cove to commune with God. And I'd tell her how long I had waited for the right person to share the cove with. We would hug. There would be peace, for a while.

What I neglected to mention was that I had previously played the same song and used the same cove to keep the peace with twenty other women. The fourth dance I added after I started to make good money as a writer; I could give them a credit card and send them shopping.

You see I would look inside myself for something to give these women and there was nothing there. All I had was my vaudeville act. There was no me.

The day would come when they would be sitting in the nest one more time needing some sign that the whole thing wasn't a sham. But my performance was over. I was out of songs, and I was out of dances.

Once past the initial encounter, seduction, and fort building, I always knew this day was coming in every relationship. I dreaded this day. This was the day the truth was out. This was the day we both knew there was something wrong with me. This was the day we both knew I was "fundamentally bad, inadequate, defective, unworthy, or not fully valid as a human being." They wanted something from me, and I had nothing to give. This was the day I knew I hated them.

I was incapable of telling anyone what was actually going on because I really didn't know what was going on. I only knew one thing for sure: this relationship was over. I couldn't live with anyone who found out my secret. I couldn't live with anyone who had witnessed my shame.

My goal now became "drive her out." Before I began I might move us to a new residence, but I made sure she picked out one she liked. You see, I knew she was going to be living there alone, and I figured if she liked the place, it would be easier for her to end the relationship. My favorite weapon for driving someone out was silence. I just stopped talking and stopped fucking. At this point there was external confirmation that nobody lived in my body. Eventually, she had to end the relationship or kill herself. I'd look into her eyes as I left and that look would still be there, but there were no sparks. I felt afraid. I didn't understand.

After I'd been in therapy a couple years, I asked Margie what the goal was, where were we going? She told me that the work I was doing was going to take me to a place in time where I would experience sexuality and tenderness in the same instant. I got very quiet. Then I got very pale. After a few moments, she asked me her very favorite of all questions, "How does that make you feel?" I told her, "First, it makes me wonder if I will ever be able to get an erection again. Second, it puts me in touch with the fact that all of the collapsed beds, broken kitchen tables, destroyed chairs, plaster knocked out of walls with heads and feet, dented car hoods, carpet burns on knees and butts that I thought had been caused by passion were in fact caused by anger!" The ladies and I had been trying to hurt each other.

The truth was out. What I was looking for in their eyes during that first encounter was repressed anger toward men in equal portions to my repressed anger toward women. Openly angry women frightened me. It was imperative that the anger be hidden and repressed, like so many Southern women I have met with honey and peach blossoms dripping off the barrel of the Uzi – which, I might add, is being held waist high and is pointed slightly down. The only reason I single them out is because the control and oppression applied to them by men and tradition is staggering. The free human being, the free woman in them is flattened almost at birth. And for most of them, the role they are forced to play is totally opposite to the truth of their feelings. I can hear the feminists screaming, "The free human being, the free woman in most women is flattened at birth." I know. I agree. It's just that in the South, it seems more blatant.

I was six or seven years into therapy when I started to uncover all of the beatings that my mother gave me before I was five and a half. I missed so much school my first year they wouldn't give me any grades. Once these beatings were out into the light, I learned that the reason I was so terrified of the anger of women was because the moment they would get mad, for any reason, I would perceive it as a real threat, a physical threat; I was going to get hurt. I would do anything or give them anything to stop their anger.

The reason I was frightened when I would look into their eyes at the end of the relationship was that they were still angry. I, on the other hand, had gotten some of my anger out through withheld sex and through silence.

Once the relationship was over, I'd take a short break and then I'd start looking for HER again. I was convinced that if I could just find the right woman everything would be okay. I absolutely didn't know the defects in the relationships had anything to do with me. The exception to that was one time about a year before I started therapy. It was Christmas Eve and I was watching the Osmond family Christmas show with a buddy of mine. My wife at the time was out of town on a trip. About half way through the show, I started to cry, and

I turned to my friend and said, "I'll never be able to have that (a happy family), and it breaks my heart." We told a few jokes and changed the subject.

To me the perfect woman was someone with whom there would be no conflict. She would never complain and never have needs that I couldn't fill, which ostensibly meant she wouldn't have needs. I knew what she looked like: she'd be tall, blond, with long terrific legs, a nice tight round ass, and small firm breasts. I knew she would have that look in her eyes, and when her eyes met mine the sparks would fly. I knew I would come upon her sometime when I was out driving around. Occasionally, I would drive around at four in the morning just to look for her. I was alone, and I hurt. I didn't know I hurt. I had an ache, a longing, that I couldn't identify. I knew she would be wearing a long, clinging, white silk gown and that she would be standing next to her white Rolls Royce. I knew she would take one look at me and say, "Come along with me, I'll take care of you." I knew I would go. I knew everything would be all right.

What I didn't know is that the HER I was looking for lived inside of me. SHE is that magic combination of God, the inner child, my intuition, my feminine part, and the truth. SHE is the mother my inner child and I always wanted. SHE is what recovery from being an adult child/co-dependent is all about. SHE is the self-love and the self-nurturing. The search was for me, not SHE.

The longer I continued to do my family-of-origin work, the more improvement I've noticed in my relationships. I have been married seven times, five times prior to therapy, two times (counting my current marriage) since therapy. Therapy began almost nine years ago. I have been married to Tina since August 1987. The other marriage, marriage number six, lasted less than a year, the entire relationship including marriage lasted about two years. When I went to the altar for marriage number six, I knew it was something I didn't want to do at the time and had told my partner so. However, there were extenuating circumstances (not pregnancy) that made the marriage a practical action at the time. My second marriage ended by annulment. My fifth marriage ended with the death of my wife.

The seven marriages should make more than a few of you want to throw the book away and discount or discard everything I've written so far. In fact, if you've continued on to this point, I'm impressed. Adult children from alcoholic and dysfunctional families/co-dependents need their heroes, mates, and themselves to be perfect. When they find a flaw in a hero, they throw him or her away. Guess who else they throw away when they find a flaw?

During the nine years since I started therapy, I ended one relationship because the woman had too much sexual anger for me. Another ended because the woman was a compulsive shopper, on my money. I gave her a choice to get some help with the compulsive shopping or call it quits. She called it quits. The end of another came when we knew we had been put together for a short time to help each other out, and that it was time to move on. She was the first to recognize that our time was over and that it was time to move on.

During marriage number six, my mate became physically ill. After about two months, she came to me one day and said "I feel distance between us."

Now I always react like a mature adult when confronted. I think I said something like, "How can you feel distance? I'm standing two feet in front of you."

She went on to tell me how she felt alone, felt as though I wasn't there for her.

I listed all the things I was doing: taking her to doctors, going to the pharmacy, going to the store, cooking, and so forth.

She pointed out that those were custodial chores, chores we could hire somebody to do.

When confronted, I can't always get in touch with what I feel, so I told her I was going to the other room and I'd respond as soon as I knew something. About five minutes later, I came back into the living room with tears in my eyes. I told her she was right. There was distance between us. I told her that the last time someone I cared about got sick, they died. I told her that a little guy inside didn't think he could take that kind of pain again, and he had put on his running shoes and took off when she got sick and that what she was getting from me was the best and all that I had to give at that moment. I told her if she needed more, she was going to have to look to her friends, her sponsor, her minister, or her therapist.

For the first time in my life that I wasn't able to deliver what my mate needed I didn't have to hate her. I didn't have to convince her that she wasn't feeling what she was feeling and didn't think I was "fundamentally bad, inadequate, defective, unworthy, or not fully valid as a human being."

There were two whole people standing in that room, one with needs and the ability to express them, the other because of the pain of past experiences, knowing he couldn't fulfill them. I had come a long way.

CHAPTER 8

"Did Onto Others"

The good news, bad news is that the alcoholic, dysfunctional family issues are multigenerational.

Good news: When I started to work on forgiving my parents, the buck didn't stop with them. They were the recipients of something that had been handed down to them, cafeteria style, from one generation to the next; that knowledge made the earlier stages of forgiveness easier.

Bad news: My two daughters by my first marriage, my one stepdaughter and two stepsons by my third marriage, and everybody else who crossed my path were next in line. I filled their trays.

If they have received no new child-raising information since their own childhood, adult children will become one of three types of parents.

Type A: They know what was done to them as children was wrong, and they swear never to do it to their children.

Type B: They think what was done to them was perfectly

okay. They think they had it coming. They pass it on without a second thought.

Type C: They can't remember what was done to them. They have repressed their childhood. Whether or not what they are doing is right or wrong, functional or dysfunctional never crosses their mind. They too pass it on without a second thought.

From the type A parents I have talked with, worked with, and spent time around, I found they are best described by the control-release cycle of the shame-bound person that is so clearly laid out in *Facing Shame* by Fossum and Mason. They resolve never to do to their children what was done to them – control. The stress of life builds up. The children behave like children, not like little adults. When the rigidity of control becomes too much, the parent releases. This comes in many forms: yelling at the child, hitting the child, hitting the mother, taking the family on a terrifying hundred-mile-an-hour ride, getting drunk, and so forth. Whatever form the release takes, it only serves to further shame the parent. The parent then vows to exercise more control so that "it will never happen again." The hopelessness of the cycle is easy to see. Nothing is going to change until the parent changes. The parent changes by cleaning up his family of origin, his unresolved issues with his own parents.

The type B parents are much more difficult to reach. They have suppressed their childhood or split off from it. The suppressed ones think their parents were perfectly wonderful. The split off ones will say things like, "Yeah, my old man beat the shit out of me, but I was a little bastard. I had it comin'."

Sometimes the type C parent can be easier to reach than the type B. The type C hasn't formed any opinion one way or the other about childhood and can't remember it. When provided with information about functional and dysfunctional, a type C can sometimes see the validity of the information and therefore isn't so quick to have to defend his or her earlier parental actions.

There are two primary reasons all three types need to

control the children. First, controlling, oppressive parenting is all they have known. Second, they all see the behavior of the children as a reflection of themselves: good child, good parent. The main ingredients in the definition of good are controlled, obedient, and quiet. They will sometimes allow the "hero" child a tiny bit more leeway but not much. If a hero is given behavior latitude, they will keep the hero in check by never allowing the "hero's" accomplishments to be good enough to get complete parental approval.

I'm a type C. I didn't remember much. All I knew was I wanted my daughters to smile at me, love me, make me proud, obey me at all times, and not embarrass me in public.

Notice how my thoughts consisted of what I wanted them to do for me. As far as I was concerned, my responsibilities ended with providing housing, food, and clothes. Not having received any nurturing, I didn't know anything about giving nurturing.

The fact that I couldn't remember most of my childhood didn't for one moment diminish the amount of dysfunction I had to hand out. The steam table in front of me was full, and I had more than enough scoops, serving spoons, spatulas, and tongs to start filling my daughters' trays when they showed up in line.

There was very little, if any, conscious thought to my actions. In fact, there were very few actions. My daughters were greeted by reactions, and I couldn't have predicted what they would be. I was being controlled by an unseen force.

"Good little children are seen and not heard," was the motto of my childhood. And for the short time they were with me, it was the motto of my daughters' childhood.

I feel terrible as I sit here writing this realizing that I didn't know anything about nurturing, that I didn't know how to provide my daughters with a sense that they were valuable, special, and wonderful.

My oldest daughter was with me until she was five; she caught the most of it. The youngest was with me until she was two; she still got too much.

My mother beat me in order to get me to stop crying.

By beaten, I mean being hit in the face, head, and neck. I had a very short tolerance when one of my daughters would cry. Now at this time, I had no memory of the beatings, I just KNEW that their crying was wrong and bad. I would shout at them, put them in their room, or spank them to get them to stop.

Although I thought I was doing a good job of parenting, in reality I was effectively breaking their spirit and teaching them to stuff their feelings out of fear of physical punishment. The legacy was passed on.

Not long after our divorce, my first wife remarried. Her new husband wanted to adopt the girls, and I gave permission. I was three years off drugs and alcohol and starting to realize I didn't have a hell of a lot to give to anybody.

With the exception of seeing my younger daughter once about thirteen years ago, I hadn't seen or communicated with either one of my daughters in twenty-three years until recently. Five months ago my youngest daughter contacted me. She had been in a relationship with a young man who had to give his daughter up for adoption as a result of divorce. This has given her a different point of view about what happened to her. After having been the little sister all her life, she is thrilled and delighted to be Alexandra's big sister. I have no idea what kind of a relationship we can develop. I have no reality of her being my daughter. She has no reality of my being her father. I am excited about finding out where we go from here. We have talked about not knowing what we want from the other. We have discussed feeling an attraction, a need to proceed.

A half-dozen years ago I was privileged to be a witness to an exchange between a mother and daughter. The daughter in her mid-twenties was celebrating her first year free from chemical addiction. Her mother, who had four years free from chemical addiction, called her on the phone. The mother explained to the daughter that she didn't have any money to buy her a present. Then the mother proceeded to give the daughter what she, the mother, regarded as a meager present. She said to her daughter, "Look, on this your first birthday, I want you to know something. I want you to know that I am responsible for most if not all of the problems you have in your life today. I'm responsible that you don't know how to take care of your children and because of that they reside with your father, my ex-husband. I'm responsible that you have so little self-esteem that you don't even know how to take care of yourself. I'm responsible that you can't hold a goddamn job. I'm responsible that you don't know how to be a friend or have a friend. I'm responsible that you can't have anything that even approaches a meaningful relationship with a man, and God knows what else I'm responsible for. But on this your first birthday, please, for your sake, understand you are the one responsible for the solutions to those problems. I did it to you, but I can't fix it." Far from a meager present. No amount of money could've bought a present as wonderful as that. For an adult raised in an alcoholic or dysfunctional home that exchange is as close to the gift of life as you can get.

I never fully understood why I was there when that took place. As the years have past, I've shared the story with as many people as I could. But I still felt that mother-daughter exchange hadn't had the impact on my life it was intended to have. Five nights ago I was able to have a similar exchange with my youngest daughter from my first marriage. She has been in therapy working hard, finding answers to her own current and past problems. I was able to confirm for her what she already suspected. She didn't have a chance. Her first two years were with me, her drug-addicted, alcoholic father. Her next sixteen years were spent in a rigid, controlling religion, not her choice. I told her it was okay to blame me as long as she needs to and to get as mad as she needs to. I let her hear me accept the responsibility for her lousy first two years. She opened the door for me to begin sharing with her the tools I have used to help me. There's hope for both of us.

Next in my life came three terrific stepchildren. By this time, I was five years into recovery from chemical dependence. This was marriage number three.

I was excited. I was going to have a family. I was going

to be able to do for my stepchildren the things that hadn't been done for me. Notice I was now starting to get a sense that my childhood could've been better. The truth was starting to seep out, and all I had done to this point was stay off the chemicals

I was going to be able to be a better husband than I had been in the past and a much better husband than my father had been. More truth starting to seep out. I couldn't have given you any specifics at this time other than my father's drinking.

What I didn't know was that I was far more emotionally prepared to be a stepchild than I was to be a stepparent. There were a hell of a lot of mornings I wished my wife would pack me a lunch and let me go off to school with the children. I didn't have any tools for the job at hand.

With the older boy my anger and violence came out. He wasn't behaving like I wanted him to. He wasn't dressing like I wanted him to. He wasn't doing anything I wanted him to. So when he raised his voice to his mother I had the excuse I needed to hurl him across the room against a wall. Or if he lied to one of us, I had the excuse to grab him by the shirt and shake him back and forth and scream at him. He was, and as far as I know still is, a bright, talented young man. But in those days he had all the problems any creative teenager has fitting in, especially fitting into the school system. At that time, I still believed that it was my fault that I had gotten poor grades in school and had been thrown out of high school. It never entered my mind that it was the fault of a dysfunctional system. So if my failures in the system were my fault, then my stepson's failures in the system were his fault. He never had a chance; he had been raised by two chemically addicted parents before he wound up with me.

My stepdaughter was in between the two boys in age. She was and, as of the last time I saw here, is a beautiful girl. She was artistic and talented. She could play guitar and sing. She was full of fun and conflicts. When she wasn't in school, she spent a lot of time with her music. I'm grateful she had her music because I had no idea what to do with her or for her. I was incapable of giving her the kind of nurturing that adolescent girls need as they vacillate between being a mature young woman one day and a little girl in your lap the next. My needs were that everybody be the same yesterday, today, and tomorrow. Her constant changes put me off balance. I didn't know whether to ask her for a date or pull her in a wagon. I think I would've been much more comfortable doing one or the other as opposed to being stuck in the middle in the roll of stepfather which, as badly as I wanted it, I didn't know what to do. I wanted desperately to be a good stepdad, and there I was without tools for the job.

At least the youngest boy and I were able to throw baseballs and footballs and build model tanks together. I got him interested in sports at the YMCA. He loved it. The focus was on sportsmanship instead of winning. The downside was that he didn't find a lot of sportsmanship at home. When we would build tanks, I would usually build the bigger, more expensive one, which he was never allowed to play with. If we built identical tanks, I made sure mine was put together better and painted better than his. I was in competition. I didn't know about nurturing, encouraging, helping, or sharing.

My prayer is that the three stepchildren and my two daughters get to do their family-of-origin work, that they can let themselves get as mad at me as they need to in order to find their own freedom. Wherever they are, I wish them all the best that life has to offer.

CHAPTER 9

"Care and Feeding"

The first fifteen years of my life were from 1935 to 1950. Very few people knew about the "total person" concept, and my family wasn't among them. They knew nothing about mind, body, and soul being a package that needs to be cared for equally. They knew nothing about seeking good health care. And in those days anybody talking about nutrition and exercise was considered part of the lunatic fringe. As a result, I had no idea how to take care of myself. On top of that, because I had no self-esteem, I didn't think I was worth the effort. I was ashamed of me. Taking care of me would've been a waste of valuable time, time that could have been used taking care of others, time that could have been used to participate in compulsive addictive behavior.

Up until a few of years ago, the only time I went to a dentist was when the pain was so bad I couldn't stand it any longer. The only time I ever saw a physician was in an emergency room.

On the occasions when I found myself in a dentist chair,

the dentist would invariably tell me that if I didn't start taking better care of my teeth, I would lose them long before their time to go. I would listen intently. They would scare me. They would demonstrate the proper systematic method for brushing. They would demonstrate the proper way to floss. I would take the special toothbrushes and floss and go home, where I would floss for maybe two weeks and brush three times a day for maybe a week longer. Then it was back to no flossing and brushing once or twice a day in a haphazard fashion.

I didn't get sick often, but, when I did, I could take a simple cold and ignore it until my temperature was so high and I was so sick that the emergency room was my only hope. They would warn me about not resting and taking care of obvious signs of illness. I would listen intently. They would scare me. I would go home, take my medicine, and get well. Then I would do it all over again a couple of years later.

When people would ask me, "How are you?" when it was one or two days prior to my mad dash to the dentist or emergency room trip, I would answer, "I'm fine, okay, no big deal, nothing to worry about, I've turned it over." I couldn't have told them I was sick and afraid and needed help. I didn't even let me know I was sick and afraid and needed help. I thought being sick, afraid or needing help was a sign of weakness. And as soon as you found out I was weak, you would know that I was "bad, inadequate, defective, unworthy, or not fully valid as a human being," and you would throw me away.

Later would come the hammer with the following engraved on the handle: "If I had worked a good enough spiritual program, I wouldn't be sick and my teeth wouldn't be rotting!" I bludgeoned myself and helped others to bludgeon themselves with that hammer numerous times.

Getting sick was not an attention getter when I was a child. One of the three or four events from my childhood that I could remember prior to therapy was having the measles. I was put in a dark room and left there alone. My mother would bring in a meal, and I wouldn't see her again until she brought the next meal and took out the dishes from the previous meal. I never saw my dad once during this time. So it isn't difficult to see why getting sick was never in my script. I didn't know you could get attention. If I did get sick and someone tried to look after me, I became very uncomfortable. Having never experienced anyone looking after me, I didn't know what to think, what to say, or how to act. I didn't know what was expected of me in return, but I did know that whatever it was, I wouldn't be able to deliver. I would have to make taking care of me such a project that the person would have to stop.

The first time I ever went to a dentist as a child I was ten or eleven. My mother found a dentist that gave her a cheap price. He examined my teeth and said they were fine. A few months later a second tooth came straight out through the side of my gum right above a dead baby tooth that should've been removed. Mother made sure that no more money was ever wasted like that again. The next time I saw a dentist, I paid for it. I was in my mid-twenties and had to have an abscessed tooth removed.

During the first five to eight years that I was no longer killing myself with chemicals, I still didn't know anything about the total person concept. I was perfectly content with the accomplishment of not taking drugs or drinking alcohol. I had plenty of other addictions and allergies to feed. I launched myself on a campaign of stuffing myself with nicotine, caffeine, sugar, salt, grease, processed food, red meat, and anything else that would help me stuff the feelings. Then, over the next couple of years, I began to see, read, and hear about people who take care of themselves. This gave me something to do. I would constantly trash myself. Jael Greenleaf points out in one of her workshops that adult children from alcoholic and dysfunctional homes constantly beat themselves up for not having skills, social and otherwise, they were never taught.

In April 1973, the middle of my eleventh year free from drugs and alcohol, someone I loved much more than I knew how too, died from cancer. When she was told her options, she refused all toxic forms of treatment. If the treatment could kill her, she didn't want it. We began seeking people involved in the nontoxic treatment of cancer. She and I were heavy red meat eaters, serious coffee drinkers, and two and a half to three pack-a-day smokers. Without exception, everyone we dealt with in the nontoxic treatment field insisted that red meat, caffeine, sugar, and cigarettes be eliminated immediately. She complied. She was willing to try anything that wasn't toxic. Unfortunately, it was too late. By the time the cancer had been discovered, it had already spread too far. She was a great lady. I have good memories of us. There are and probably always will be moments when I miss her.

At one point during the three months from the time they told her she had cancer until she died, I too tried to give up the red meat, coffee, sugar, and cigarettes in order to be supportive. I woke up one morning and said, "If she can give them up so can I." By noon of that day there was serious seismic activity taking place inside my body and brain. I thought I was going to explode like a fragmentation grenade. By three that afternoon people who knew me were strongly suggesting that I have a cup of coffee and a cigarette. I looked like a man possesed. Not only was I starting to show the signs of the physical withdrawal, the suppressed feelings were starting to surface. I had no idea what was going on. I felt crazy as a loon and wanted some relief. I had a cup of coffee and a cigarette followed by a ton of shame because I had failed my dying wife; I had let her down. It never dawned on me that I had followed in the family tradition of letting me down. Today when I look back at me, that thirty-nine-year old man who was in the middle of circumstances he absolutely didn't understand, I praise me for just trying, for making the effort.

A week or so after she died I was sitting in a restaurant having steak, coffee, and cigarettes. I looked at the meat and thought, "I can give this up." Over the following week I gave up red meat. Pork was harder than beef. Sausage, bacon, and pork chops were favorite foods. I know now it's the salt and grease in pork that made it harder to give up. In the fifteen years since, I have had red meat twice. Once a young lady I was living with and I went to her girlfriend's for dinner, and the friend had prepared a pot roast. The young lady I was with didn't want to hurt her friend's feelings, so we ate it. The second time was about a year ago here in New Mexico at a sweat lodge, at a dinner given to celebrate the success of a couple of friends who had been Elk hunting. I got sick both times.

About a year after my wife's death, I gave up coffee. I had been trying to for a while and had gotten to where I was drinking half regular coffee mixed with half decaf. I was a serious coffee drinker. I had the percolator plugged into an electric timer so it would turn on and be ready by the time I got up. I didn't want to stand around waiting for it, too stressful. I got up one morning and went to drink my fresh cup of half caffeine half decaf, and my throat closed. It was as if a small hand reached up and squeezed off my pipes. I tried a couple more times to get the coffee down, but it wouldn't go. My body was saying, "You have drunk your lifetime supply of coffee, too bad you're only thirty-nine years old."

I made a cup of straight decaf and swallowed it without a problem.

In the next weeks and months I was proud of myself; I didn't eat red meat, and I didn't drink coffee.

Although I had given up coffee, I hadn't given up caffeine. I switched to diet colas, mainly Tab. The amount of caffeine in each can was much less than in an equal amount of coffee. I would get up in the morning and have a bottle of Tab with a cigarette. I thought everybody found Tab, Rice Crispies, milk and sugar compatible tastes. Just as with coffee, I would have a can of Tab and a cigarette before going to bed. It never did whack me out and wire me up like coffee had, even though on particularly stressful days my Tab consumption would run upwards of eighteen cans. It had to be okay; my throat wasn't closing.

Six years after my wife died I was at Suicide Prevention in Los Angeles researching a story on adolescent suicide. Some of the workers and the then head of Suicide Prevention and I gathered in a small conference room. I whipped out my pack of Marlboros and my latest electronic butane lighter and set fire to my cigarette to stuff down the nervousness. Looking around the room, I noticed there wasn't an ashtray in sight. I thought, "Oh, oh, unfriendly turf." The people couldn't have been nicer. One of the workers went out into the next room to get me an ashtray. From where I sat, it sounded as though he was remodeling the outer office. Drawers opened and closed, closet doors opened and closed. Finally he came back with a platter big enough to serve a fish.

While I tried to nonchalantly flick my ashes into the platter, the head man told me that they had an official opinion on cigarette smoking, and would I be interested in hearing it? My inner child answered "yes" before I had a chance to think about it. Children hate smoke. He told me that now that the scientific proof was in that cigarette smoking of and by itself could take your life – they viewed cigarette smoking to be a form of covert suicide. I immediately envisioned a little tiny gun with a little tiny bullet. Extremely uncomfortable with that little piece of information, I quickly got the material I needed for the story and left.

I would like to tell you that from that day on I never smoked again. But that wouldn't be true. The truth is the next six months were miserable. Every time I lit a cigarette, I would hear the gun go off. On particularly paranoid days, I would look around to see if the people next to me had heard the gun go off. Did they know I was blowing my brains out one puff at a time?

At the end of those six months it had become more desirable to me to be a nonsmoker than a smoker. I went to Smokenders with two friends. I needed a program and the support of friends in order to quit. Others just get up one day and say "ENOUGH" and toss the pack. Each person has to find what works for him or her. I and one of the two friends I went to Smokenders with still don't smoke. It has been ten years. The other friend never was able to quit. A couple of years later he relapsed back to drug and alcohol addiction and has since taken his life. I am not trying to make a connection between cigarette smoking, relapse, and the end of his life. I am simply stating the facts.

At the time I quit smoking, I was in the middle of a separation from my then wife. I had lost control and desperately wanted it back. She was sleeping with somebody else. I wanted her back, control back, and him out of the picture. On top of that I was getting to be a little difficult to be around. The tiniest things would make me angry. I am convinced one of tar and nicotine's primary functions, besides killing us, is stuffing anger.

One day Harold quits smoking. A couple days later he comes home from work, still not smoking. Entering the living room, he looks at the green sofa against the wall and then at his wife Martha. He looks back at the sofa and then back at Martha. Finally he says to Martha, "I hate that puke-green sofa!"

Martha, shocked, says, "Harold, that sofa has been there for twenty years!"

Harold says, "I know, and I've hated it for twenty years!"

Martha says, "I think you ought to have a cigarette."

A smoker who uses cigarettes as one of the methods to stuff his or her feelings is surrounded by friends and family who are accustomed to that behavior. When the smoker quits and the feelings start coming up, everybody gets uncomfortable. People perceive this change in the smoker as a threat and don't hesitate to encourage the smoker to go have a cigarette.

I read somewhere that in this country cigarette tobacco is cured in sugar. If that's true, it sure would explain what happened next; I couldn't get enough sugar. I made the Cookie Monster on Sesame Street look like a calm, rational critter.

I treated my sugar addiction as I had my drug addiction. I tried to convince myself it didn't exist. I would sit at home at night, and a voice would say, "There's no ice cream in the house." I would answer back by telling the voice it was okay. I didn't need ice cream, I would be able to be like the rest of the people in the world and have a glass of water and go to bed. I thought I was the only one fighting sugar. Ten fifty PM would roll around and I would be out the door breaking my previous record to the carport. I would drive seventy miles an hour to 31 Flavors where I would broadside to a stop in the street, leap from the car, and rush into the store before they could lock the door. I would buy a quart of pralines and cream, a jar of butterscotch topping, and a jar of dry roasted cashews.

Back home I would get a bowl, and I don't mean a chicken-shit little cereal bowl – I'm talking about a real bowl, a mixing bowl. With bowl in hand I would proceed to make a sundae, using most of the ingredients I had just purchased. Within a half hour of consuming the sundae I would slip quietly into a sugar coma and pass out on the couch, successfully having fed an addiction and stuffed my feelings one more time.

It wasn't long before I weighed forty pounds more than I had when I quit smoking. And it wasn't long after that I bought a pair of pants with a size forty waist. The day after I bought the pants I couldn't get them fastened, and that was the moment of truth. I said to myself, "You can eat all the sugar you want. You can have sugar morning, noon, and night if you want. But these are the biggest pants you're ever going to own."

Someone suggested eating a red delicious apple every time I wanted sugar. It worked. I probably ate ten to twenty apples a day the first couple of months, but the pounds came off slow and steady. After the age of thirty, you don't want the pounds to come off fast. The elasticity in the skin has started to go and, if you lose weight too fast, you wind up looking like you're standing in a sack.

The first twenty-five pounds melted away. I started to feel good about not eating red meat, not drinking coffee, not smoking, and not eating sugar. But other rumblings were starting to go on inside of me. I was crying more. I was aware of anger. I was aware that sometimes things people said or did hurt me. I was afraid. I wasn't sure God was going to help me out anymore. In fact, I started to interpret the emerging feelings as separation from God. So, on one hand, I was starting to take care of myself and, on the other, I was frightened. It was three months later that I started therapy.

A couple months later a friend came to me and suggested that I start running. He felt that it would help me stay off the cigarettes, lose the rest of the weight, and feel even better. I had tried running once before when I was still smoking. It didn't last long. I ran out of breath after such a short distance that I was embarrassed to run where anyone could see me. Doing well wasn't enough – I needed desperately to look good.

Out came the running shoes, shorts, and T-shirts. This time I had my friend and a couple of others to run with, so even though I felt silly, their presence made it somewhat okay. I would just suck my stomach in and run as hard as I could when there were strangers around. Running my ass off to impress people I didn't know and would probably never see again was a waste of good energy.

As I stated earlier in the book, thanks to a lot of injuries acquired while I was drinking and drugging, my body isn't exactly straight. After a couple of weeks of watching me bob, weave, and hobble down the running paths, my friend suggested I go see a sports medicine podiatrist and get some orthodics made for my shoes. If I could get my feet going straight ahead, I would be able to run farther, faster, and easier. My friend recommended the best sports medicine podiatrist in southern California. Unfortunately for me, he was located in Long Beach, which was about thirty-five or forty miles from where I lived.

At this time in my life I would drive you to Long Beach to see the best doctor, but I wouldn't drive me that far. I went to a podiatrist in Century City, a ten-minute drive from where I lived. The podiatrist made incorrect orthodics and, less than a mile into my run, my back went out.

Now my friend recommended the best sports medicine chiropractor in the country, a chiropractor who was working with the Olympic team. But this guy was in Pasadena, which was as far for me to go as Long Beach. I would've driven you to Pasadena. I, on the other hand, went to a chiropractor in Marina del Rey, a five-minute drive from where I lived.

He was twenty-five pounds overweight, smoked, and didn't know anything about running. One treatment and my back was worse.

I was having the same success with close-to-home, cut-rate doctors that my mother had had with the dentist.

After stumbling around bent over for a week, I finally got in the car, hunched over the steering wheel, and in agony drove myself to Pasadena.

My friend was right. The chiropractor in Pasadena was terrific. After the third treatment, I was upright and feeling good. Then the chiropractor told me to go see the podiatrist in Long Beach.

Three days later I was in the car, on the freeway, and on my way to Long Beach. As I started to get close, I began to have an uneasy feeling in my stomach. It was a sensation I was starting to associate with discoveries about to fall on me in therapy. Thinking there was no correlation between therapy and a foot doctor in Long Beach, I pushed on.

Sitting in his office in that chair with my legs and feet straight out, I was frightened. It was more than just the fear of a new situation.

The doc came in, said, "Hi," and immediately picked up my right foot and started turning it in every direction. He asked "What happened to your feet when you were a kid?"

I said, "Nothing that I know of, why?"

He said, "Your right foot lays on its side, it's practically a club foot."

I said, "Maybe I was born that way?"

He said, "No, this is a type of structural problem that is caused after birth."

I wanted to throw up and didn't know why.

I kept the conversation on the subject of running while he finished the exam and made the molds of my feet. I didn't want to talk about my feet when I was a child and didn't know why I didn't want to talk about it. I just didn't.

On my way home in the car I was sick to my stomach, sad and angry, and didn't know why.

I had been home about an hour when the phone rang.

It was my mother. She had just come from her podiatrist and was complaining about how he had done a lousy job of cutting her toenails.

I said, "As long as we're on the subject of feet, what happenend to mine when I was a kid?"

She proceeded to tell me nothing had happened. But an unknown force (the inner child) kept me prodding her. Finally she told me I had very high arches when I was a child and had to wear very expensive shoes. She must have repeated that the shoes were expensive at least six times.

After I got off the phone, I started pacing like a madman. I was sick to my stomach, sad, angry, hurt, felt betrayed, and didn't know why. I was up all night.

Luckily the next morning was a standing appointment with my therapist. I brought her up to date on what had just happened the day before. We took the feelings of sadness, hurt, betrayal, and anger over my feet and traced them back.

I found me at two and half years of age standing in a hallway. I had tears streaming down my face. I was pointing to my right foot and telling my mother that the shoe was too small; it hurt.

She placed her index finger in front of her lips and said, "Shh, not so loud. Your father will hear, and he'll get mad."

I went to the studio and called the foot doc in Long Beach. I asked him if wearing shoes designed for high arches that were too small could've turned the foot over?

He said, "Yes, absolutely. That was probably it."

The pain of truth was excruciating. They wouldn't even buy me shoes that fit.

To this day one foot is a full size smaller than the other. Often, in order to be comfortable, I have to buy two pairs of shoes, one pair size nine and one pair size ten. I used to buy nine and halfs and grin and bear it.

It took me a few years of sadness and anger to get past that one. Then eventually, when I started to work on forgiveness, I could only wonder what kind of doctors my mother's parents took her to, if they took her to any. And what kind of shoes did they make her wear?

With my new orthodics and my new one size ten and one size nine running shoes, a-running I went.

During the first ten years after my wife died, I would occasionally enroll in a gym in an attempt to improve my condition and conditioning. I deserve a lot of praise for that. I have a belief system that tells me that I shouldn't go to a gym until my body is perfect. These efforts would last maybe ninety days, then I would miss a day. Missing a day to me meant failure. Then I would be ashamed, and I'd trash myself for not being able to stick with it. And, believing that nobody else ever missed a day, I wouldn't go back. Or if I did, it wouldn't be long until I missed another day, and that would finish me. I must have enrolled in a dozen different gyms in the second ten years of my recovery from chemical addiction.

There was a lot of stress in going to the gym. First, a lot of the girls and women were lifting more weight than I could. And I still had the old jailhouse, iron pile, mentality of "he who lifts most is the best human being." It was embarassing as hell to come up to a machine after some tiny damsel had just finished and not be able to move the weight until I had lightened it. On more than one occasion, when I would see a gorilla coming down the line of machines behind me, I would increase the weight by a hundred pounds when I finished. Anything to look good. Just being there exercising to improve the quality of my life wasn't enough. Second, I didn't like my body. It wasn't perfect. I was ashamed. I thought that in order to be okay I should look like Mr. America. I did not have the ability to give myself praise for having the courage to risk the unknown process of taking care of myself. Third, I expected myself to know everything there was to know about exercise. I thought I was defective if I had to have the instructor explain it to me. And if I didn't understand it after the first demonstration, I knew I was a failure.

Adult children from alcoholic and dysfunctional families often suffer from a learning impairment. After all of the yelling, screaming, beatings, mixed messages, lies, triangulation (communication through third parties), and absence of approval, it's no wonder many of us have a hard time focusing and retaining information that is being presented to us.

IT'S OKAY IF SOMETHING HAS TO BE DEMON-STRATED TEN TIMES BEFORE YOU UNDERSTAND IT. IT TAKES WHAT IT TAKES. A good instructor understands that and will work with you until you have it right. Bad health club instructors are like bad therapists, because of their own inadequacies, they rush you to your destruction.

Today I can usually make someone demonstrate something until I understand or realize that I never will. But back in December 1983 that wasn't the case. I worked all year getting ready to run my first marathon. Because of my discomfort in health clubs, I had purchased a weight bench and did my upper body and leg-strengthening exercises at home. I had picked the Honolulu marathon because I love Hawaii and I had heard it was the best first-time marathon for runners.

I arrived in Honolulu two weeks early so I could get used to the humidity. The word was that the humidity caved in a lot of marathoners who weren't used to it. I arrived in Honolulu alone. Although two weeks before I left, I had just met a very beautiful, very sexy lady; I didn't have to bring her along. This trip was for me and the inner child. It was our marathon. We had worked hard getting our running mileage up until we had run twenty-two miles the last two times before leaving California. We had had to fight tremendous battles with the inner adolescent who always wanted to chase after the young girls when we were out running. Fortunately, he wasn't fast enough to catch them. God, how he hated being in a forty-eight-year-old body. You know who the inner adolescent is, guys! He's the part of us that's locked in an emotional and sexual time warp. He likes fast cars, squeezing big breasts in cashmere sweaters and hates having his hair mussed up. He's the one that gets you to cruise the high school on the way to work while you tell yourself you're doing it to make sure there are no sexual deviants around. My inner child and I used to do our laps and speed work at Beverly

Hills High School. I had a great yardstick to tell me what kind of day I was going to have. If the girls in the gym classes looked like beautiful young ladies preparing for young womanhood, if I could think about them being teenagers and going to dances, having fun – I knew it would be a good day. If they looked like potential dates – I knew I was in for a long day with the adolescent in the driver's seat.

The kid and I were ready. We knew we could do it.

I called around Honolulu until I found a health club that would let me work out six times in the next two weeks and just pay them for the six times – another first for me. I didn't have to keep my mouth shut and enroll for ninety days just so I could work out six times.

I walked into the health club, and it was a meat market. All of the pretty bodies were there, and the best bodies were on the instructors. There were a half dozen male and a half dozen female instructors. The guys had twenty-inch waists and belonged in swimsuits on the cover of G.Q. The girls were perfect; they all had the word staff embroidered over their left breast. And what they hadn't been able to accomplish with the machines, they had accomplished with the aid of plastic surgery. My adolescent was in seventh heaven. He still thought he had a twenty-inch waist and could bench press two seventy-five. The room was filled with Nautilus equipment. I had never seen Nautilus equipment.

I was finished. The combination of my adolescent needing to look good and my belief system telling me that when I don't know something I'm flawed guaranteed disaster. I straightened my back, stuck out my chest, and strutted over to the machine that looked the closest to my weight bench at home. I got on it with my legs in the wrong position and proceeded to do the first leg curl. I felt the knee go before I was half way up.

I spent the next two weeks in the hotel nursing the knee. I ran the marathon. The knee went out eighteen miles in. I had it bandaged at an aid station and limped, skipped, hopped, and sort of ran the last eight miles. I finished! I went straight from the finish line to the emergency hospital. A few months later I had knee surgery. This time I picked an expensive close-to-home doctor. I never went for a second opinion. He screwed it up, and I'll have to have it done again one of these days. Today, I bicycle instead of run

After the knee surgery, I needed to return to a gym for rebuilding. I picked the YMCA in west Los Angeles. It was terrific – everything I needed and no meat market atmosphere. A lot of senior citizens worked out to improve the quality and length of their lives. And a lot of people who were serious about good health. I learned working out at the Y that even though I felt silly, it didn't mean I looked silly.

The areas of care and feeding are where most of us who are adult children from alcoholic and dysfunctional families subject ourselves to tremendous abuse. I believe learning about and participating in good nutrition, exercise, and preventive medicine is essential to recovery from the devastation of our childhoods. Like all of the process, it comes down to finding out what is functional for you: walking, running, swimming, bicycling, exercycle, Pritikin, Fit for Life, macrobiotic, vegetarian, meat market, YM/WCA, home equipment, Nautilus, Universal, free weights, yoga (my preference is Hatha yoga), or a combination of any of these recovery tools. We must learn that we aren't weak and flawed because we need rest and a certain amount of sleep. We must learn to find a good dentist and a good preventive medicine doctor.

When I first moved to New Mexico I called three people I knew and asked them for a dentist. All three are adult children from alcoholic families. None of them would recommend the dentist they were currently seeing. Their dentist was good enough for them, but not good enough for a friend.

Learn to always get second and, if necessary, third opinions. If you can't do these things alone, and many of us can't, find a supportive friend who will go with you and help.

Don't be surprised if any sudden interest you show in your health is perceived by the people in your life as a threat.

CAUTION: compulsive, obsessive people can take nutrition and exercise and turn them into rigid, unbending, controlling, compulsive, obsessive dances of death that continue to cut them off from their feelings. If you have set a diet, exercise, rest, sleep regimen for yourself and the first time you miss a beat you want to kill yourself, you may want to lighten up.

There are some areas I'm very rigid about. I don't drink anything with caffeine, alcohol, or sugar in it. I don't eat red meat, chicken, or anything with sugar or honey (my body can't tell the difference). I alternate between periods of being a vegetarian and periods where I add fish. For sweets I eat fresh fruit or bakery goods sweetened with fruit juice. When I first got off sugar, I wouldn't eat anything that resembled bakery goods. After a while, I let myself have some treats made with sorbitol, but I had to give sorbitol up because it created tremendous gas. I don't eat dairy products, but occasionally I'll have a vegetarian pizza or a salad dressing with cheese in it.

I gave up dairy products in order to breathe. One night I was in my yoga class and complained about a sinus headache. My yoga teacher said if I wanted to never have a sinus headache again I should quit eating dairy products. I went into shock. Cheese was a staple. I could take three bricks of different types of cheese, a box of triscuits, a couple of leaves of lettuce and make that my dinner. At that time in my life I was just getting started running and compared to what I had been eating I considered that a very healthy meal. Anyway, I gave up dairy products, and I haven't had a sinus headache since. We're the only animal that drinks another animal's milk.

A good way to learn the foods that you are allergic/addicted to is to make a list of the foods you absolutely can't live without.

My inner child depends on me for good food, exercise (the kid loves most of it) and rest. I'm all he has to care for him. The better care I take of him, the more we trust each other. The more we trust each other the deeper our relationship grows.

CHAPTER 10

"The 'F' Word"

FORGIVENESS
rain on the parched desert
sunlight on the darkened land
smile on a child's face
the breath I take in
the song of the bird
the flower opening to the bee
food growing from the earth
single red rose
hug
tina's smile
gleam in my eye
peace in my stomach
breeze in my soul
hymn in my mind
laughter in my heart
tear in my chest
wonderful
freedom
hard

FALSE
the norm
fog in which I hide the truth
head trip
acceptable lie
sword on which I impale myself
pretend
fear
water I pour on the fire of life
guilt
mask
detour on the pain highway
bitterness on the skin
rotting of the soul
fire of hell
song of Dante
mating of the black widow
dance with a skeleton

There are two kinds of forgiveness: false forgiveness, which takes place in the mind and true forgiveness, which takes place in the heart.

False forgiveness is achieved by gathering information and coming to a logical conclusion or by simply making an intellectual decision to forgive. The decision can be forced upon you by yourself or by others.

False forgiveness is a socially acceptable method of stuffing your feelings.

False forgiveness is the method of forgiveness practiced by religion, many self-help groups, and most people in twelve-step recovery.

The need for false forgiveness is a result of fear, the fear generated in each of us when confronted with having to experience the pain and feelings attached to looking at the truth of what happened to us when we were children.

I hurry to falsely forgive you because I believe that as soon as I forgive you, you will stop hurting me.

False forgiveness is like putting a dirty bandage on an open wound. Underneath, on the emotional level, the wounds are still bleeding unattended and are being further infected by the lies contained in the bandage.

True forgiveness is a smile, a sigh, a tear, and an understanding that takes place in the heart.

True forgiveness is an acknowledgment of your pain that comes from me allowing myself to experience my pain, past and present.

True forgiveness is an act of great love, the love that I have bestowed on myself by my willingness to go to the caverns of my soul for the truth, a truth that can't be found in the mind.

True forgiveness is a gift from God that was with me when I arrived on this planet. The gift was lost in the bombing, sirens, air raid shelters, and subsequent rubble of my early childhood.

True forgiveness comes when I get rid of the belief system that says forgiving you makes you right and me wrong.

True forgiveness is not just the absence of anger.

True forgiveness is possible when I no longer believe that the moment I forgive you, I will cease to exist.

My ability to truly forgive you means that finally there is a ME.

The road to true forgiveness is defintely "the road less traveled."

I always envisioned true forgiveness coming in a grand and wonderful way. I thought that one day I would walk into my therapist's office, she would stand there smiling like a messenger from heaven, and with the voice of an angel she would say "today is the day." She would lead me slowly to the couch while I tried to figure out if our feet were actually touching the ground. I would lie on the couch, and with a wave of her hand I would be bathed in sunlight. Then before I could blink, she would wave her hand again and true forgiveness would come in a blinding flash with heavenly music playing and a hundred-voice children's choir singing outside the office door.

God, I love fairy tales.

Based on MY experience, achieving true forgiveness is a long, long, long, long, long, hard, one-little piece-at-a-time process.

Compared with the struggle I am going through in order to forgive my mother, my father was easy. He's been dead for twenty-four years. He hasn't been around continuing to do the same things. Mother, on the other hand, hasn't changed, despite the fact that I have had periods of true forgiveness. The periods last until her behavior today triggers a new and horrible memory from my childhood. The behavior can sometimes be nothing more than an expression on her face. Other times it's what she says, what she does, what she doesn't say, or what she doesn't do.

When my mother opens the door and I find myself staring into that angry, pinched-up face, my inner child runs for cover. I try to tell him she probably just sucked on a rotten lemon, but he doesn't believe me, he's seen that face all his life. And in the past that face meant he was going to get hurt.

When I put my arms around her to hug her, hold her, she's stiff, unresponsive, and uncomfortable. Sure, part of me knows that obviously there was no physical affection shown in her family. But the other part of me is hurt. And when I'm hurt, I'm angry, and when I'm angry, I'm not in forgiveness.

She'll serve me foods she knows I don't eat and in the process of setting it down in front of me will say, "I know you don't eat this, but it's okay." NO, IT'S NOT OKAY! My kid inside cries and dies a little every time she does it. It's an old pattern: what's important to him, his feelings, and his needs are not important. When I am in her presence and this is going on, I am not in a forgiving place. Sure, on an intellectual level, I understand that her parents obviously didn't care about what was important to her, her needs or her feelings, but that doesn't change what I am feeling at that exact moment. It's this constant Ping-Pong action between intellectual knowledge and internal feelings that convinces me, for now, forgiveness is something that comes in inches and seconds.

I think a lot of people say, "I forgave my parents every-thing," in hopes that their children will forgive them every-thing. And if they find themselves angry at their parents after they have made this proclamation to the world, they deny their own anger. Now, under the guise of forgiveness, they are doing to their feelings what their parents did to their feel-ings. They are also hoping that by denying their anger, their children will deny their anger. Then everybody can walk around being nice to each other while pretending the past didn't happen. It's better for me to skip sainthood and be who I am and feel what I feel.

Three things keep me going back to my mother's for more: one, I operate under the great cosmic myth that if she and I stay alive long enough and if I go back often enough, she will change; two, if I keep going back often enough, she will stop being threatened by the changes in me; three, guilt.

A few weeks ago I really got in touch with an eye-opening truth about my inner child's relationship with my mother.

I was going to be doing a workshop in San Diego so I had made arrangements to go visit Mom. I was going to pick up a rental car at the airport and drive up and visit for a cou-ple of hours. As the plane got closer to San Diego, I started to feel uncomfortable. After getting off the plane and head-ing for baggage claim, the discomfort increased. I decided to use a little fantasy trip routine I use when in doubt. I closed my eyes and imagined myself going to the counter and rent-ing the car. Then I imagined myself finding the car, putting in my bag, and heading off down the freeway toward Mother's. I almost threw up.

I decided I wasn't going. I took a pass on the rental car and grabbed a cab for the hotel.

Suddenly on the way to the hotel my inner child started saying, "I want my mommy. I want to go see my mommy. I want to see my mommy. I want my mommy."

I thought "Oh, oh, I blew it. I better have the cab turn around and go get the rental car." But intuitively I knew I should keep riding in the cab while I sorted this out. I asked little Bobby if he was sure he wanted to go see his mommy.

He said, "Yes." I asked him if he was absolutely sure. He said, "Yes." There was still something that wasn't right. I asked him if he was ready to go back to the airport, get a car, and drive north to my mother's house. He said "NO, I want MY MOMMY!"

At that moment the light went on. I realized that he didn't want to go see my mother. He wanted to go see the mommy that he wished he had had. He wanted to go see the mommy that was going to greet him with hugs and kisses, the sparkle of love in her eyes, and a warm welcoming smile on her face. He wanted to go see the mommy that thought he was special and that the things he did were wonderful. He wanted to go see the mommy that was proud of him. He wanted to go see the mommy that would fix him foods that he liked to eat. He wanted to see the mommy that would hug him back when he hugged her. He wanted desperately to see THAT mommy.

I took him to the hotel where I spent some time with him in the mirror. I looked in his eyes and told him how special he was, how much I loved him, how proud I was of him, and that I'd take him to eat food he wanted to eat. Then I called my mother and told her I wasn't coming.

I lied to her. I told her that the airlines had lost some of the equipment I needed to do the workshop and I would have to stay around San Diego until it was located. I didn't want to tell her that the thought of coming to visit her made me want to vomit.

My mother and I have never sat down and discussed any of my discoveries about my childhood. She has idealized my alcoholic father and our lives together. My therapist is convinced that my mother has the truth of what went on buried so deep that she can't remember any of it. As of this writing I am in agreement with my therapist. But I have also reached a place where I am having a great deal of difficulty determining how to deal with my mother. I could reinforce the old "protect the parent at all cost" belief system; I could practice the "it doesn't help me to hurt the ones that hurt me" theory; or I could do what I need to do for my own recovery, my own freedom.

The majority of professionals who work with adult children from alcoholic and dysfunctional homes seem to be divided into two camps: (1) It doesn't help to hurt the ones that hurt us; (2) Confront the parents and have it out once and for all. There is a third group, the minority, that believe that each person must find which way works for him or her. Luckily for all of us, the third group is growing rapidly.

The first group believe we should say what we need to say either to an empty chair, to someone playing the part of one of our parents, in group therapy, or in private therapy.

Up until very recently I have felt that not hurting the one that hurt me was the right way to go. That has put me, however, in the position where I have to lie, which makes me very uncomfortable. This last lie in San Diego didn't sit well with me. But because I took time to find out which mother my child wanted to see, I was able to say things to my mother that I hadn't been able to say before. I was able to tell her how bad I felt that I wasn't able to come, how disappointed I was that I wasn't able to come, how badly I wished that I could come visit. What I didn't tell her was that the situation existed because of her behavior, not because the airline lost some equipment.

At this moment I don't know where the dividing line is between hurting me and hurting my mother. I know that, thanks to sitting down and writing this book, I am ready to begin peeling off another layer of oppression; the thought of that doesn't thrill me. Part of me says, "No, no. No more crying that hard. No more being that angry. No more hurting that bad." But I know it's time.

Perhaps by the time I've worked with a therapist and taken off the next layer, I will know what my next move is to be where my mother is concerned.

Intuitively, I believe that, after the next layer of oppression is off, I am going to have to start communicating some of my feelings to my mother. There is no way I can do that without some of it hurting her. But, as it is, it has to hurt her that she sees her son maybe once a year and the rest of the time he is a victim of unfortunate circumstances. Then again, maybe it doesn't hurt her. In the last nine years she hasn't been willing to make the effort to come to see me. Until two years ago, it would've been a seventy-five mile train ride. On the other hand, on more than one occasion, she has been able to fly from California to Colorado with my stepfather to visit his sisters. My therapist Margie always said forget what they say, pay attention to what they do.

What I've tried to do here is let you see my confusion when it comes to having to deal with and forgive a parent who is still alive, unchanged, and exhibiting abusive behavior.

Before I started this book, I thought I would wait until I had this area of forgiveness resolved before I began writing. Then one day I realized that to do that would be practicing co-dependent behavior – an unwillingness to let you see me until I had everything worked out so that I would look good.

I support the group of therapists who believe each of us has to find out what is functional for us – confront the parents, don't confront the parents; tell the parents some of what we are feeling today, tell them nothing of what we are feeling today.

From the time I started working on my family-of-origin issues until now, I feel I have almost always done what was functional for me at the time. Now I am starting to feel that what has been functional in the past may no longer be functional today. This is why I feel there is no place for rigidity in the recovery process where co-dependence issues are concerned. What works one day will not necessarily work the next.

As I change, my needs change. In order for me to recover, I must continue to honor my changing needs.

Our society and your family will give you tons of support when it comes to not confronting or sharing your feelings with your parents. Society and your family will pat you on the back for "making nice." You will receive applause for visiting the old folks regularly when they wind up in the rest home. If applause isn't enough, you can get awards for taking them in and letting them spend their last few years with you.

Society and your family will not support you for confronting, sharing your feelings, refusing to visit, or refusing to house the old folks.

The chant usually goes something like this: "Visit, visit, visit, it's your duty." It's a rare occasion when someone takes into consideration that maybe the reason the children don't visit is because the parents have been terrible parents. Perhaps the parents have been guilty of sexual, emotional, and physical abuse. And, in too many cases, this abuse is beyond the comprehension of most of us.

If you try and make the argument that they were lousy parents, society will say, "Bitterness over things in the past doesn't help anybody." Life is a hell of a lot more than a book of rigid rules, hundred-year-old, irrelevant clichés, and nostalgia for days gone by.

To say that bitterness doesn't help anybody is to say that you don't matter, that your feelings don't matter, that you should think only about the feelings of the other person. This is a classic definition of co-dependence. It is saying that it's unimportant when you find yourself face to face with this old person in the rest home that you feel wrong, dirty, afraid, inadequate, abused or that you want to hit, cry, vomit, or flee. And that these feelings are the result of the old person's past and sometimes current behavior. Many of those old folks continue to be abusive long after they've been put in a rest home and right up until they draw the last breath.

Just because two people had sexual intercourse doesn't contractually bind me to be nice to them for life. Parents do not deserve respect simply because they are parents. Respect is something everyone has to earn, including parents.

I know a lot of people who have disrupted their whole lives in order to be close to their parents during the parents' last few years. Often the only thing wrong with this great sacrifice is that they hated their parents.

If my kids hate me when I'm in the process of winding

down, I don't want them forcing themselves to come and visit. I don't want that kind of energy around me. I don't think that guilt-motivated actions are good for anybody, the giver or the receiver. Also, I think it's a slow death when we sell out our feelings by being nice to people because we are afraid of their anger. And most of these dysfunctional parents will verbally beat the hell out of you if you don't honor their every wish in their last years.

At least where my mother is concerned I don't go nine out of the ten times that she tries to put pressure on me to come. That's not a perfect hundred percent, which I may never achieve, but it's a hell of a lot better than the ten out of ten times I use to go. And on those trips I was filled with hate and self-hate on the trip going, while I was there, and on the trip home. I hated her for the past, the present, and for her power over me. I hated me for selling me out and for giving her the power.

How will I handle it when my mother can no longer take care of herself? I don't know.

Now as far as I can tell, my dad lays completely forgiven in a veterans cemetery in southern California. After I had been in therapy for about five years, I started to feel a need to clean it up with my dad. The feeling got stronger and stronger over the next couple of months until I finally went to the cemetery on a cold, very windy afternoon.

I spent two and a half or three hours there with my dad. I went from standing, to walking around the grave in circles, to sitting crossed-legged on the ground, to kneeling and back again. I went from quiet conversation to shouting, to tears. I went from wanting to dig his skeleton up, grab it by the ankles and slam it up and down on the headstone, to regretting that I never got to talk to him from the time I got off drugs and alcohol.

I was surprised to find that my inner child had a lot of compassion for my dad. He was sorry that my dad had never been able to have a relationship with him. He was sad that my dad never got to know his son. My inner adolescent turned up for this occasion, and he too was far more understanding than I had expected. He too was sad for my dad because he never got to know his teenage son. The inner adolescent and the inner child figured my dad must have had it pretty rough when he was a kid. When the three of us were finished with our sadness, anger, regrets, and compassion, it was time to say goodbye.

I looked down at the grave and explained to my dad that the little boy and the teenager were coming with me. I told him it was a shame he had blown it as a father and missed it all. I told him I felt sad that he had had his own empty, painful childhood. I told him that it was now up to me to take care of the inner adolescent and the inner child. I shared with him how their nurturing and love were my responsibility now and that I was excited. I assured him that we would never completely forget him. With the tears streaming down my face, I took the hands of my inner adolescent and my inner child, and we started to walk to the car. After a few steps, the tears stopped and the three of us began to skip.

The process of trying to forgive myself has been as hard as trying to forgive my mother. I'm still here. I'm still doing many of the same things to myself.

I've been able to forgive myself for a lot of past behavior but not all of it. I still haven't forgiven myself for picking incompetent people to manage my money. I still haven't forgiven myself for not getting a college degree. Yes, even though I know how dysfunctional the educational system is, I feel like there's something wrong with me because I didn't complete it. I don't feel as if I've completely forgiven myself for being a failure as a father and a stepfather. I don't beat myself over these issues as often as I used to, but I still don't feel bathed in God's forgiveness or mine.

Maybe being bathed in absolute forgiveness, when it comes to people who are living, is a myth, a myth to help people stuff their feelings and live a conflict-free life. Or maybe total forgiveness will come when I have experienced and expressed all the feelings of anger, sadness, and hurt I have had about a person or situation. So far experiencing and expressing all the feelings have been part of a long and difficult process because I and "they" keep repeating old, hurtful behavior.

I get so frustrated when I still ignore my feelings or don't trust them or don't express them. I feel as though I've failed when I split off from myself, when I'm not present inside of myself. It would be nice if I could always give myself praise for how far I have come in these areas, but I can't. Yet my progress is tremendous. I am at least fifty percent a new person since I started my family-of-origin work nine years ago. The message is patience: to give myself time. I am trying to undo years and years and years of damage. I am trying to undo belief systems that are engraved in my soul.

Occasionally, when I start beating up on myself, I am able to stop and look at how far I have come. When I can do that, I think I start to feel what it's like to be bathed in forgiveness. I am more nurturing of myself than I have ever been in my life. Perhaps in the act of being nurturing to myself, I am forgiving myself. Perhaps on the rare occasions when my mother's current behavior isn't hurting me and I am nurturing to her — I am forgiving her, and I don't even know it. Perhaps forgiveness is moment to moment, like life.

CHAPTER 11

"A Still Small Voice"

This is little Bobby's chapter. He wanted to write his own. I am typing this up from twenty-eight hand written pages. I have not added or deleted one word. With the editor's help, a minimum amount of punctuation has been added to help make it clear to the adult reader. Little Bobby refers to me as Mom, Dad, Bob or Dad, Mom, Bob or just plain Bob. This is my inner child, and I'm very proud of him.

I want to write. I wish I could write pretty – they taught me to print in Colorado, and then I came to California and the teachers just let me keep printing they were lazy. I was used to lazy, Mom was lazy. Why Mom? Why? Why did you have me. I don't think you really wanted me. If you did want me it's really sad that you didn't know what to do with me. You shouldn't've hit me. I didn't do anything. All babies cry when they need something even love. It hurt me terrible when you hit me it scared me when you would yell at me – did somebody yell at you when you were little. I felt cold when you looked at me I felt cold and naked. I did the best I could to be quiet but I'm sorry I'm sorry you go so mad. It was wrong. I didn't do anything – It hurt when I was little and I'd run to get a hold of your leg – I needed to feel safe but you always moved away you always went to the kitchen I hate the kitchen. I can feel my dad Bob worrying that he isn't going to be able to read this – I'll help – It's okay – I get afraid hell stop me. He just promised he wouldn't stop me – I'm smiling. I want to write I have to write I want to write to the other little kids out there like me.

Hi

I'm Bobby what's your name.

I'm tired Alexandra (the baby) keeps me awake. She's teething but I don't ever want them to not hold her comfort her dont let her cry in a room alone . . .

Dad, Mom, Bob wants to help me with this. I'm writing long hand and he wants to do it on the computer but I don't know how I'm afraid he says I can talk to him and tell him what I want to tell the kids and he'll write it down on the Computer. I need to do this myself I want the kids to know that I care enough to do this on my own. Thanks anyway Dad Mom Bob.

I hope you weren't beaten when you were little it hurts awful. But being yelled at hurts awful. I saw a bumper sticker on the bumper of a car I liked – it said – "It shouldn't hurt to be a child"

It hurt when I was small I had to be very quiet – Mom always worried about me desterbing Dad or other people – really I desterbed her she didn't know what to do with me they both wished I would disappear.

Dad Mom Bob is worried because he knows I spelled disterb wrong. It's okay the kids will understand.

I guess if you weren't hurt as a kid you wouldn't be reading this book – It's those of us hurt as kids who have the need to pretend we are somebody else. Being me got me hit and ignored and hurt. So I had to be quiet and pretend not to be. . . . It's hard to pretend not to be when you are. I exist but I have had to hide.

I need lots of things I need to be held, hugged, rocked, loved, kissed, smiled at, I need to be smiled at a lot I like to be smiled at – It makes me smile inside and outside – I need to play and laugh it feels good to laugh. Mom Dad Bob I need to laugh more you work too hard I know you want to help the kids too but Im an important kid and I need to laugh. We need more bears here in the office one isn't enough even if he is big. He gets lonely – we kids know alot about stuffed animals and dolls and critters being lonely. I see the other lonely little children ever time Mom Dad Bob looks into the eyes of an adult that hurts.

That Indian we saw yesterday on his way to get money for his little plastic bag of empty Cans. He hurt – the booze had almost destroyed him but I dont hate the alcohol I dont hat the drugs I hurt when I think about how he hurt when he was before he drank – I know his little boy is just like me I know he got steped on by big people when he was little. Big people step on you with looks, with words with fists.

Im alive energetic a child of God open the gates and let me out I wont embrass anybody I promise I dont want to hurt anybody. I don't even want to hurt mom and dad any more. . . .

I want to tell the children, "I love you I love you I love you. You are special and unique." Mom Dad Bob is impressed I used the word unique – there's alot they dont know about what we know. . . . .

Mom Dad Bob is tired he wants to rest – this is hard work for him, he wants this to look right, sound right, touch people. Its hard for him to let me write – he forgets we children touch people just by being.

I want so much for all of us Children to just be – people are so afraid of us –

Telephone – I like to answer the phone most of the time especially when nice people or other kids are on the other end Bob doesn't like to answer he think it breaks the flow when he's writing – Someday maybe he'll let me teach him how to keep the flow going. He's impressed I spelled writing correctly. He usually spells it with two "T's".

People are afraid of us because they are afraid of our spontanity. Bob's hungry he's going to go eat lunch. I'll write more later —

It has been ten days since Mom, dad, Bob and I went to lunch. Just letting me write is hard on him. He has had to write another chapter before letting me finish mine – We also went and did some workshops. I like doing the workshops. I get to help Bob help the adults find us kids, I love it when I see them cry and meet the kid. And afterwords the room feels so good cause its full of kids.

For those kids who havent had the adult come find you yet – be patient they will. If they're reading this book especially this chapter it means they're looking even if they don't know it.

We have much to teach our adult. My Mom, Dad, Bob is too serious a lot of the time. I'm trying to teach him to laugh more, to have fun, he worries a lot.

I talk to God a lot and pray that he helps my Mom, Dad, Bob to lighten up. He worries about money, taxes and stuff, I tell him everything will be okay but he sometimes gets like all adults and thinks what do kids know. we know everything important. God is our constant buddy God is with us always – For a while I was afraid for Mom, Dad, Bob. People kept telling him God was a loving parent but he didn't know what a loving parent was so he thought God was like his parents and that made him afraid. If he'd asked me for help I could've helped him. We kids know what a loving parent is thats why it hurts so bad when we dont have one. And even when they buy us Clothes, and toys and take up places we know there's no love. Thats why all that stuff only makes us feel better for a minute then the hurt comes back.

I was afraid of Mom, Dad, Bob when we first met but that was because he had done terrible things to me just like our mother and father did to us. But I learned once they come to meet us they start doing better right away and we can help them by loving them. They'd love us if they knew how.

It was awful cold when I was little and it hasn't been that

cold in a long time, even when Mom, Dad, Bob forgets that Im here.

I love you out there little friends I hope soon you can come out and play soon.

I like it when there are a lot of children like me in a room.

I get afraid when Im in a room with big people who don't know they have kids inside. They are always so angry and cold and stiff. They dont cry and laugh down where I am.

But we can help. – keep kicking, and screaming and Calling out until they come looking for you. Then we can share a tear and a good laugh and we can take them to have fun.

We have a very big job but God loves us and he is with us all the time giving us the stuff we need.

I hope Mom Dad Bob lets me write more soon. I want to write a book for kids. I want to write a book about a little boy and his teddy bear who grow up in a house with a mad drunk father and a mad mommy and the little boy and his Teddy meets a little girl and her Raggady Ann doll who are growing up in a house where they buy her everything but nobody hugs her and they wont let her get dirty, Then I can show the world how much we need and how much we know —

I love you.

CHAPTER 12

"Today"

I'm excited, enthusiastic, tired, sad, happy, and reluctant to finish the book. I feel as if the minute I write the words "The End" I will fall into a deep, dark void. This book has been part of my life for the last two years. It has been the major focus of the last five months.

In the morning I hang out in bed for awhile with Tina and Alexandra. The three of us read the paper. Alexandra, five months and one week old, reads it with her hands, feet, mouth, and face. By the time she's done, she looks like she's ready to sing a duet with Al Jolson. Paper reading over, it's a fast bowl of brown rice cereal, a quick shower, and off to the office to work on the book.

I used to work at home, using the second bedroom for an office. It took Alexandra only a day or two after she got home from the hospital to move in her changing table, crib, stroller/baby buggy, diaper pail, dresser, playpen, rocking chair, and everything else she needed. Daddy was moved out.

Alexandra, having everything she needs, is another story. When Tina was about eight months pregnant, she was in a therapy group here for artists. She mentioned to the group that she was really worried about the baby being so close and our being so broke. A woman in the group told her not to worry. The woman told Tina to trust the baby. She assured Tina that the baby would draw into her life everything she needed before she came. Starting the next day, people began showing up. Some of them we knew, some of them we didn't. They brought clothes, strollers, beds, bedding, toys, pampers, everything. When Alexandra made her appearance, she had everything she needed.

Earlier in the book when I said my money issues coupled with the incompetent people I had picked to manage my money had wiped me out, I wasn't kidding. Today, I'm in a rebuilding process. There are some tough tax problems that need to be settled. And what once was triple-A credit was wiped out, so it's futile to ask me for my Master Charge.

It's a good thing I had to get out of the house and find an office. If I were home, I would spend most of my time playing with the baby, and the book would come out some time in 1990.

From the time I arrive at the office until I get home again, it's usually eight to ten hours, that includes taking time for lunch.

When I get home, it's play with the baby for a few minutes, and then it's time to eat dinner. Then, if it's not too late, Tina and I will take in a movie or something in order to unwind – me from fatherhood and the book – she from motherhood and painting. If it's too late we play with the baby a little more, then we go to bed, turn on the news and mumble a few words to each other about sleep deprivation since the baby. Occasionally, we ask ourselves if we really believe the people and the books that say sleep and sex do return to your life.

I still have a real problem with abandoning myself. I lose track of my feelings and my needs. It's as if suddenly I don't exist; there isn't enough of me to go around, and I view all of my life as projects that I am responsible for completing.

Spending time with the baby becomes a project. Spending quality time with my wife becomes a project. Spending time with me becomes a project. The book is a project. Phone calls are projects. The workshops become projects, the list goes on and on and on. And if I don't complete all of the projects immediately, I am a failure.

When Tina sees me slide into this mode, she generally tries to get me to go for a walk in the hills, just she and I and the dog – away from the baby, the TV set, the book, and so on. I'm hard to reach when I've abandoned myself, and it can take her two to five days to get me out on the trails. When I'm cut off from me, even the walk becomes a project, just one more project that I don't have the time or the strength for.

When I'm in that state, I'm convinced it's what I must do in order to finish the book on time. I have to get the book done! I have to meet the deadline! We need the money! There is no time to slow down! I'll take care of me later! I'm okay don't, bug me! Once I've got that motor running, trying to reach me and nurture me is really tough because I view the act of talking to you as a project.

Yet, reality is the chapters I have written while in that "go faster, work harder, put in more hours" state of mind, I have had to go back and completely rewrite. My best work is done when I'm in touch with me, taking time for me and my needs. And part of taking time for me and my needs always includes my wife, baby, and friends.

I spent my whole life cut off from myself and feeling like I was "fundamentally bad, inadequate, defective, unworthy, or not fully valid as a human being." I surrounded myself with people who suffered the same malady. When I initially start to lose touch with myself, it's a result of those old shame feelings churning around inside. If I have a project like the book, I focus on it. Now I have a valuable project, so I am a valuable person. I then see this loss of self as a shelter when, in fact, it's a prison – an old familiar prison. You can't get in, and I don't want out.

The difference today is that by the third or fourth day, I know I'm in prison. Then I'm reachable. In the past I spent years not knowing I was in prison. I felt better; I felt safe in my shelter/prison. Today, I feel awful shortly after the cell door closes behind me. I don't always know why I feel awful, but at least I know I feel awful.

Even though I've been working on adult child from alcoholic/dysfunction family, co-dependence behavior for nine years, I'm not cured. At least I'm not cured by my old definition of cured.

CURED (my definition): cool, calm, collected, on top of things, prepared, loved by all, superhusband, superdad, superperson, superhuman, all-powerful, all-loving, unruffled, not needy, controlled, conflict free, loved by all, capable of giving advice on any subject.

The person I'm becoming is confusing to me. When I'm into my feelings, I often judge myself as I used to judge others who were experiencing and expressing their feelings. I saw them as out of control, frightened, weak, whining and embarrassing to be with. Yet, when I would see them going about taking care of business, I considered them to be self-assured, competent, real, and their presence made me uncomfortable. Today, when I am going about taking care of business, I often see myself as self-assured, competent, real, and my presence makes others uncomfortable.

My confusion comes from my own B.S. – belief system, that is. This belief system originated in my childhood. I never understood that strength, competency, and realness come from experiencing and expressing feelings and knowing one's needs and going about getting them met. My belief system says weak people go around slobbering their feelings and asking to get their needs met. My belief system says you can get hurt going around expressing your feelings. I got hit for crying and yelled at for laughing. My belief system also tells me that strong, competent, and real people have a secret ingredient that I am missing and can never get.

I am just starting to understand that the secret ingredient is self-esteem: a sense that I am valuable, I am important, I am a child of God. Scott Peck says in his book *The Road Less Traveled* that the sense that we are valuable must be given to us by our parents when we're children. And if it's not, we are left the incredibly difficult task of acquiring it in adulthood.

In order to have self-esteem, there must be a self. Shame is the culprit. When shame is flowing around inside of me, there is no room for me. So, I step outside and cease to exist except through the eyes of others, or at least my interpretation of what I think I see in the eyes of others.

My feelings are my connection with me and with most, if not all, of my repressed childhood. My feelings are who I am. When I am in touch with my feelings I am real. I am here. I am.

I spend a lot of my life today in touch with my feelings. Experiencing and expressing feelings give me a sense of aliveness, a sense of being valuable. Sure there are times when I feel inadequate, unworthy, and overwhelmed. But, most of the time, I am able to keep moving and not allow those feelings to paralyze me emotionally or physically.

Emotional paralysis for me is walking around town like a robot with no feelings, just a tight chest, stiff neck, and very shallow breathing.

Physical paralysis is not leaving the house, not returning the phone call, not leaving the chair – frozen in time – the fear that any physical action will be the end of me, exposure of the real shameful me.

The satisfaction of being afraid and doing it anyway is tremendous. I find that if someone else is around, it's very helpful to admit to the fear. Then I don't have to look good, and it's easier to go face the business deal or get on the roller coaster or ride the elevator up the outside of the skyscraper.

A great freedom comes from not having to know everything about everything and being able to say I don't know and from asking questions when I don't understand.

A lot of times my feelings still scare me. Sometimes I fall into the lie that, if I start crying, I won't stop. Yes I will, just as soon as I'm done. Sometimes I look at my wife or my daughter, and the feelings of love and caring start to shoot so deep down inside of me that it scares me. That's uncharted territory down there. But when that happens, I remind my-self that, where my feelings are concerned, it was all uncharted territory when I started therapy nine years ago.

Being a dad is terrific, frightening, and occasionally over whelming. When Alexandra is crying and I'm holding her, trying to comfort her, an alarm goes off inside of me and says, "That's it, your crying time is up." This time span is usually three to five minutes. The moment the alarm goes off, I start to tighten up. I want her to stop crying now. I could throw her against the wall to stop her. I have no intention of throwing her against the wall, and I have no intention of submitting her to the kind of terrible energy that is taking place inside of me. I pass her to my wife. I'm convinced children pick up feelings. If Tina is reaching the end of her rope, we will call Mary, the wonderful woman who babysits for us, and give her the baby while we flee the house. This leaves Alexandra comfortable in the arms of someone who sings Spanish lul-labies to her. Alexandra loves Mary; she lights up every time she sees her. Tina and I want her to love Mary. We want her to be able to love others. There is no threat to us if she loves her sitter, because both of us have had to work so hard to learn to love someone that we don't want Alexandra to have to go through that.

I realize that the built-in time limit on my daughter's cry-ing is a legacy from my mother. I figure I was probably al-lowed to cry three to five minutes before I got hit. I am learning a lot about my own childhood just by paying attention to my reactions to Alexandra.

I also have found that sleep is important. When I have enough sleep, I have more patience with Alexandra. When I'm short of sleep, I am more easily overwhelmed.

I can't speak for younger couples, but for those of you who are in your mid-thirties to early fifties thinking about hav-ing a baby, I would suggest you make sure you love each other a lot.

Tina and I are thrilled that we have Alexandra, but at times, the baby puts tremendous stress on our relationship. It is an emotionally demanding, time-consuming situation.

We have to learn our parenting skills as we go. We have to talk to the experts and read the books. Many times we have flown blind and trusted our intuition. Now, trusting our intuition always works out fine, but the action is filled with doubt and is exhausting.

In the hospital all the nurses knew that Tina was a first-time mother and that I had no reality about being a father. When it came time to go home with the baby, the nurse that carried Alexandra out to the car said to Tina, "When in doubt, trust your intuition." If we've had enough sleep, we both find that our initial intuitive response to Alexandra is to nurture her. Then our childhoods jump up and say, "If you pay that much attention to her, you'll spoil her." We go with our intuition. Now, if we haven't had enough sleep, our initial response is to take an ad in the paper offering a female Anglo baby for sale.

There is a wonderful trade-off taking place in this whole baby-nurturing process. Many of the things Tina and I learned to do in order to nurture our inner child, we do for Alexandra. Many of the things we are learning to do for Alexandra, we then are able to do for the inner child.

Just stopping taking drugs and getting sober didn't make us good parents. And I think we're good parents. We have had probably twenty-one years of therapy between us, all of it aimed at putting us in touch with our feelings and teaching us to experience and express those feelings. We love our daughter very much, and we want her to experience us as real people, full of feelings – people who are occasionally in conflict with each other but don't have to stop loving each other, because they understand nobody has to be wrong. We hope we can provide for her a sense that in this home, she is always safe and always loved. That no matter where she has gone and what she has done, we love her. We may not approve, but we don't want her to think that our love is contingent on our approval.

I know a number of people who have been raised by parents who were in recovery from chemical addiction, and they're having real trouble with their lives today. What confuses them is that they think because their parents stopped drinking and drugging, they were good parents. If the parents didn't do their own family-of-origin work and didn't learn new parenting skills, they probably did a job very similar to the one that was done to them.

One of the things that's very important to me today is getting the information out about the reality of what it's like for most people who were raised in alcoholic and other dysfunctional families. I am convinced these are the issues that cause the alcoholic to drink, the addict to take drugs, the overeater to eat, the work alcoholic to work, the recovering person to relapse, the sex addict to seduce, the depressed person to take his or her life: the list goes on and on.

If you were to walk up to me today and say "Okay, my life is less than satisfactory. I don't think I'm happy. In fact, actually I feel I am fundamentally bad, inadequate, defective, unworthy, and not fully valid as a human being. What should I do?"

I would suggest the following: If you know there was alcoholism in the family, attend a minimum of six meetings of Adult Children of Alcoholics Anonymous. The organization is referred to as ACA or ACOA. If you can't get a listing from your local phone company, try calling the local offices of Alcoholic Anonymous or Alanon; they might give you meeting locations. If they don't have the information, try calling your local treatment facilities that deal with alcohol and drug treatment. They may be able to give you the information you require.

It's possible you might find the first ACA meeting unsettling. Most of us who come from alcoholic or dysfunctional families are not used to the open expression of feelings. We have a tendency to view people who express their feelings in public as mentally ill. This is Bull Shit, provided by our belief system.

If you don't think there was any alcoholism in the family, then I would suggest you try going to a minimum of six meetings of Co-dependence Anonymous. This organization is referred to as CODA. Use the same locating techniques as

above. If there are no CODA meetings in your area, then
attend six ACA meetings. The alcoholic family is just one of
the many various dysfunctional families. The end results in
the children from all dysfunctional homes are pretty much
the same.

Group therapy is also an excellent recovery tool, as we
are basically ashamed of ourselves and the group sharing is
very good for us. You can find groups that are designed to
deal with alcoholic or dysfunctional family issues by contact-
ing a local therapy referral service, if your community has
one, or by asking people who are attending ACA or CODA
for referrals. Also, you could call your local treatment centers
to see if they have a referral list. If the center tries to talk you
into coming in for immediate in-patient treatment, tell them
you'll get back to them after you've had a chance to look
around and talk to some people. After you've gone to a few
meetings or begun work with a therapist, you may decide
you need to do some immediate, intense work. Then start
asking around and find out which facility has the best in-patient
programs.

If for one reason or another groups don't appeal to you,
then individual therapy is more than adequate. I believe it's
imperative that you find a therapist who is dealing specifi-
cally with the issues of adult children from alcoholic families
and/or co-dependence. You need a therapist whose method
of treatment will put you in touch with your feelings and help
you experience the feelings from your childhood. The most
desirable and beneficial situation is to work with a therapist
who has firsthand experience with the issues. As a rule, you
can only go as far in your family-of-origin work as the therapist has gone in his or hers. Trying to go further can usually
create stress in the client-therapist relationship, ending with
your being made to feel that there is something wrong with
you.

Don't be afraid to quiz a therapist about his or her experience with the issues. You have a right to request a free
twenty-minute get-acquainted session. You have a right to
like your therapist, and you have a right to feel safe – not safe

on the intellectual level – but safe in the stomach. The mind will most likely feel threatened. It will fear exposure. Exposure under therapy guidelines is how we get free.

Go to workshops designed to help inform you about the problem. Go to workshops that will provide you with some tools to help you work on recovery. These workshops will be the ones designed to help put you in touch with yourself or workshops designed to introduce you to your inner child and teach you methods for maintaining communication with the inner child. Look for reasonably priced workshops run by people who have experience in the issues.

There are workshops that do a lot of guided imagery. I have mixed feelings about their value for people who aren't already down in the basement (i.e., in the process of digging out the old rotting foundation and building a new one). I think often these workshops can be more frustrating than helpful. If you've been tearing out the old foundation and building the new one for a while, then guided imagery can be a great tool to teach you to take time to stop and smell the flowers.

There is a suggested reading list in the back of this book. All of the books suggested have some good information pertaining to adult child and co-dependence issues. Give yourself permission to read books with the understanding that you take out of them what feels right to you and ignore the rest.

If you've already met your inner child and aren't sure what to do with the child, buy some books on parenting. They're great for helping you continue your relationship with the inner child. You will find the better books in your local New Age bookstore. You know the one – the one run by hippies.

Today, I live without having to spend hour upon hour looking for people to blame. Somebody had to be at fault, nothing just happened.

Today, I can listen to your opinion without being threatened by it and without having to make you wrong if it differs from mine.

Today, a lot of people consider me a controversial

speaker. I think what they are trying to say is what is true for me isn't true for them.

Today is life. Today is all there is, and for most of my life I wasn't here. Life was what was happening while I was busy making plans, getting ready, wondering what you were thinking.

Today, I don't have to make myself hate the old in order to enjoy the new.

Today is okay. I'm here today, present, and accounted for.

Today my life is filled with teddy bears. My inner child loves them, and he has quite a collection. In fact, he has so many that last Christmas I had to go around the house and ask the bears which ones wanted to volunteer to go to a home for abused children to be put under their Christmas tree. About forty-five bears volunteered. It was quite a ceremony when they said goodbye to my inner child and the other bears.

Today, it's fun to watch how accepting people are of grown women on airplanes with teddy bears and how quiet they get when there's a grown man with a teddy bear.

Today, my wife and I can argue. We laid the groundwork by reassuring each other that we love each other and will not abandon the other physically or emotionally because of anger. It's hard. The conversations are exhausting but worth it. There is no choice.

Today is a hell of a lot better than any time prior in my life – definitely better than nine years ago when I was living in my penthouse wanting to die.

Today, I can allow my wife to be who she is and do what she does without being threatened by her actions.

Today, my wife and I find other adult children to go play with.

Today, I understand I have the right to surround myself with supportive people.

Today, I avoid people who are abusive.

For a guy whose whole life use to be pretense, today is quite good. Finally, somebody's home in my body, and that somebody lives in freedom most of the time.

Freedom is the ability to be who I am and to stop showing you characters that I create on the spot. It's the ability to express my feelings, trust my feelings, to let you see my feelings. "It's me being me and letting you see me."

Today, sometimes, I still find it scary to tell someone what I really feel about people, places, situations, what I like, what I don't like, where I want to go and where I don't want to go, where I want to go but am afraid to go.

Today, when my wife and I pray, we sit in bed in the morning and hold each other and talk to God like children. This is after years of dozens of different types of meditations and religious practices.

Today, I try hard to follow Wayne Kritsberg's (author of *The Adult Children of Alcoholics Syndrome*) advice and not mistake human kindness for co-dependence. If in doubt you'll always know afterwards. If it was human kindness, you will feel good. It it was co-dependence, you will feel ripped off.

Today occasionally we go to a nondenominational church where, at the end of the service, the minister asks, "Are the children ready?" At that moment the doors in the rear of the church open, and all of the nursery school and Sunday school children march down the aisle to the front of the church. As the children come down the aisle and line up in the front of the church, the entire congregation sings to them. Alexandra loves it; she smiles and laughs while Tina and I cry.

Today, Tina and Alexandra are part of my life. Tina has seen more of me than anyone, outside of my therapist. Hopefully, I can show Alexandra enough of me to assure her she's okay.

At fifty-two I am finally evolving rather than revolving.

Once there was a book review in *Time* magazine on a book that had to do with death and dying. The picture that the staff artist drew for the review was one of an old person, hunched over in a chair, against a backdrop of flowered wallpaper, waiting to die. The shadow on the wall is the child inside the old person sitting up straight with his or her arm thrown over the back of the chair, looking around at the world. It is that child, that spirit inside of me, that I try to honor today.

The truth about your childhood and its effect on your adult life will set you free.

I hope this book has shed some light on the path you will take to meet yourself.

Suggested Readings

For Your Own Good by Alice Miller, Farrar Straus Giroux

Facing Shame by Fossum and Mason, W.W. Norton & Co.

Adult Children of Alcoholics Syndrome by Wayne Kritsberg, Health Communications

Adult Children of Alcoholics by Janet Geringer-Woititz, Health Communications

The Grief Recovery Handbook by John James, Harper

Lost in The Shuffle by Bob Subby, Health Communications

Models of Love by Barry and Joyce Vissell, Ramira Publishing

Codependent No More by Melody Beattie, Hazelden

Codependence Misunderstood, Mistreated by Anne Wilson-Schaffe, Health Communications

The Family by John Bradshaw, Health Communications

Choice Making by Sharon Wegscheider-Cruse, Health Communications

Healing the Child Within by Charles Whitefield M.D., Health Communications

Flying Boy Healing The Wounded Man by John Lee, Health Communications

Young Alcoholics by Tom Alibrandi, CompCare